Wide Angle

3

WORKBOOK

KRISTIN DONNALLEY SHERMAN

OXFORD
UNIVERSITY PRESS

OXFORD
UNIVERSITY PRESS

198 Madison Avenue
New York, NY 10016 USA

Great Clarendon Street, Oxford, OX2 6DP,
United Kingdom

Oxford University Press is a department of the University of Oxford. It furthers the
University's objective of excellence in research, scholarship,
and education by publishing worldwide. Oxford
is a registered trade mark of Oxford University
Press in the UK and in certain other countries

ACKNOWLEDGMENTS
Back cover photograph: Oxford University Press building/David Fisher
Illustrations by: Aaron Sacco/Mendola Artists pp. 61.
*The Publishers would like the thank the following for their kind permission to reproduce
photographs and other copyright material:* **123rf:** pp. 62 (Interview/Antonio Diaz),
66 (Thinking head/Setsiri Silapasuwanchai, **Alamy:** 34 (Woman packing/Lev
Dolgachov), 37 (cyclist/Wig Worland), 55 (Shop window/Juliane Thiere), 58 (Hotel/
Cultura Creative), 80 (Worried Woman/Kobryn Andrii), **Blink:** Cover/ Edu Bayer,
13 Man w/ Brain moniter/Edu Bayer), 35 (Teddy bear and pillows/Nadio Shira
Cohen), 68 (Cosplay/Gianni Cipriano), 70 (Man bookshelves/Gianni Cipriano),
76 (man with magnifying glass/Gianni Cipriano), 78 (schoolgirls/KrisAnn Johnson),
84 (family and horse/Gianni Cipriano) **Bridgeman Images:** 38 (Gogh, Vincent
van (1853-90) / National Gallery of Art, Washington DC, USA). **Getty:** 5 (women
talking/Hero Images), 9 (urbanruin/ApMadoc),10 (Treadmill0Katarina Premfors),
19 (Interview/Steve Debenport). 40 (Photographer/Jordan Siemens),44 (driverless
car/Karen Bleier), 44 (driverless car/Karen Bleier), 56 (Shopping bags/Britt Erlanson),
59 (teacher/Hill Street Studios) **Getty/iStock:** 3 (Girl pointing/RistoArnaudov),
24 (PeopleonStreet/JordiRamisa), **Oxford University Press:** 73 (book cover/OUP)

Shutterstock: 14 (Papyrus plant/Jerry Lin**),** 16 (Lab Rat/ Vasiliy Koval), 27 Male
athlete/Bbernard), 41 (Selfie/Sergey Noikov), 42 (Blurry photo/7th Son Studio),
45 (Flyingcar/Costazzurra), 48 (Ant/Andrey Pavlove), 49 (Grasshopper/Nednapa),
69 (person with Laptop/Frank Peters),83 (Woman disusted/Michal Kowalski),
Superstock: 2 (Grandmother/Erickson Productions Inc), **Tinkersbubble.org:**
31 (Tinker's Bubble house/David Spero).

Authentic Content Provided by Oxford Reference

*The author and publisher are grateful to those who have given permission to reproduce the
following extracts and adaptations or copyright material:*
p.3 Adapted from *The Oxford Companion to Medicine (3 ed.)* by Stephen Lock, John
M. Last, and George Dunea. Copyright Oxford University Press 2006 http://
www.oxfordreference.com/view/10.1093/acref/9780192629500.001.0001/acref-
9780192629500-e-283?rskey=udx2ke&result=6;
p.7 Ralph Waldo Emerson in *Oxford Essential Quotations*, edited by Susan Ratcliffe.
Copyright Oxford University Press 2017 http://www.oxfordreference.com/
view/10.1093/acref/9780191843730.001.0001/q-oro-ed5-00004155?rskey=WPhXBE&
result=7;
p. 10 Adapted from *Food and Fitness: A Dictionary of Diet and Exercise* (2 ed.) by Michael
Kent. Copyright Oxford University Press 2016 http://www.oxfordreference.
com/view/10.1093/acref/9780191803239.001.0001/acref-9780191803239-e-
379?rskey=7KUxS1&result=8;
p.14 Georgie O'Keefe in *Oxford Dictionary of American Quotations* (2nd ed.) edited by
Hugh Rawson and Margaret Miner. Copyright Oxford University Press 2008 http://
www.oxfordreference.com/view/10.1093/acref/9780195168235.001.0001/q-author-
00008-00001232?rskey=0KGjAo&result=37http://www.oxfordreference.com/
view/10.1093/acref/9780195168235.001.0001/q-author-00008-00001232?rskey=0KG
jAo&result=37;
p.17 Adapted from *Dictionary of Animal Behaviour (2 ed.)* by David McFarland.
Copyright Oxford University Press 2014 http://www.oxfordreference.com/
view/10.1093/acref/9780191761577.001.0001/acref-9780191761577-e-
219?rskey=U6gqQv&result=6;
p.21 Nelson Mandela in *Oxford Essential Quotations* (5th ed.) edited by Susan Ratcliffe
Copyright Oxford University Press 2017 http://www.oxfordreference.com/
view/10.1093/acref/9780191843730.001.0001/q-oro-ed5-00007046?rskey=4p7UYa&r
esult=1;
p. 24 Adapted from *A Dictionary of Travel and Tourism* by Allan Beaver
Copyright Oxford University Press 2012 http://www.oxfordreference.com/
view/10.1093/acref/9780191733987.001.0001/acref-9780191733987-e-
5858?rskey=VV1PBB&result=25;
p. 28 Robert Maynard Hutchins in *Oxford Dictionary of American Quotations*, edited
by Hugh Rawson and Margaret Miner. Copyright Oxford University Press 2006
http://www.oxfordreference.com/view/10.1093/acref/9780195168235.001.0001/q-
author-00008-00000812;
p.31 Adapted from *The Oxford Companion to Architecture* edited by Patrick
Goode. Copyright Oxford University Press 2009 http://www.oxfordreference.
com/view/10.1093/acref/9780198605683.001.0001/acref-9780198605683-e-
1277?rskey=kgsn1K&result=9;
p. 35 Louisa May Alcott in *Oxford Dictionary of American Quotations*, edited by Hugh
Rawson and Margaret Miner. Copyright Oxford University Press 2006 http://
www.oxfordreference.com/view/10.1093/acref/9780195168235.001.0001/q-
author-00008-00000025;
p.38 Adapted from *Encyclopedia of Aesthetics* (2 ed.) edited by Michael Kelly
Copyright Oxford University Press 2014 http://www.oxfordreference.com/
view/10.1093/acref/9780199747108.001.0001/acref-9780199747108-e-
558?rskey=boBSEz&result=22;
p. 42 Jean Luc Godard in *Oxford Dictionary of Quotations*(8th ed.) edited by Elizabeth
Knowles. Copyright Oxford University Press 2014. http://www.oxfordreference.com/
view/10.1093/acref/9780199668700.001.0001/q-author-00010-00001361;
p.45 Adapted from *The Oxford Companion to the History of Modern Science* by J. L.
Heilbron. Copyright Oxford Univeristy Press 2003 http://www.oxfordreference.
com/view/10.1093/acref/9780195112290.001.0001/acref-9780195112290-e-
0665?rskey=11DOim&result=10;
p.49 Albert Einstein in *Oxford Dictionary of Quotations*, edited by Elizabeth Knowles
Copyright Oxford University Press 2014 http://www.oxfordreference.com/
view/10.1093/acref/9780199668700.001.0001/q-author-00010-00001079;
p.52 Adapted from *The Concise Oxford Dictionary of Politics and International Relations*
(4 ed.) Copyright Oxford University Press 2016 http://www.oxfordreference.
com/view/10.1093/acref/9780199670840.001.0001/acref-9780199670840-e-
1655?rskey=RxEVEA&result=1;
p.56 Bill Bryson in *Oxford Dictionary of Humorous Quotations* (4th ed.) edited by Ned
Sherrin. Copyright Oxford University Press 2012 http://www.oxfordreference.com/
view/10.1093/acref/9780199570034.001.0001/q-subject-00002-00000200?rskey=Mgl
AZi&result=1;
p.59 Adapted from *The Oxford Companion to American Politics* edited by David
Coates. Copyright Oxford University Press 2012 http://www.oxfordreference.
com/view/10.1093/acref/9780199764310.001.0001/acref-9780199764310-e-
0060?rskey=jbSGFk&result=10;
p.63 Diane Ravitch in *Oxford Essential Quotations*, edited by Susan Ratcliffe. Copyright
Oxford University Press 2017 http://www.oxfordreference.com/view/10.1093/
acref/9780191843730.001.0001/q-oro-ed5-00017763;
p.66 Adapted from *Encyclopedia of Aesthetics* (2 ed.) edited by Michael Kelly
Copyright Oxford University Press 2014 http://www.oxfordreference.com/
view/10.1093/acref/9780199747108.001.0001/acref-9780199747108-e-
519?rskey=wcgcug&result=28;
p.70 Neil Gaiman in *Oxford Essential Quotations* (5 ed.) edited by Susan Ratcliffe
Copyright Oxford University Press 2017 http://www.oxfordreference.com/
view/10.1093/acref/9780191843730.001.0001/q-oro-ed5-00017943;
p.73 From *Oxford Bookworms Library Level 2: Anne of Green Gables* by L.M. Montgomery
retold by Clare West. © 2010 Oxford University Press. Reprinted with permission;
p. 77 Oscar Wilde in *Oxford Dictionary of Quotations*, edited by Elizabeth Knowles
Copyright Oxford University Press 2014. http://www.oxfordreference.com/
view/10.1093/acref/9780199668700.001.0001/q-author-00010-00003431;
p. 80 Adapted from *Oxford Encyclopedia of the Modern World* edited by Peter N.
Stearns. Copyright Oxford University Press 2008 http://www.oxfordreference.
com/view/10.1093/acref/9780195176322.001.0001/acref-9780195176322-e-
504?rskey=oSBAWM&result=8;
p.84 *Oxford Dictionary of Proverbs* (6th ed.), edited by Jennifer Speake. Copyright
Oxford University Press 2015 http://www.oxfordreference.com/view/10.1093/
acref/9780198734901.001.0001/acref-9780198734901-e-1226

Contents

1 Interactions

Simple present and present continuous ▶1.1

1 Choose the correct words to complete the sentences.

1 Lilia *admires / is admiring* her art professor.
2 We *discuss / are discussing* your suggestion now.
3 I *don't like / am not liking* working around a lot of people.
4 Workplaces *change / are changing* these days. They don't look the same as they used to.
5 Many people *use / are using* their phones for work, even on weekends.
6 My classmates and I *work / are working* on projects this week, so we don't have class tomorrow.

2 Complete the sentences with the correct forms of the words in the box.

email	spend	start	use	wait	work

1 Anton _____ his boss right now to check on the meeting time.
2 Our team meeting _____ at 10:00 a.m. on Mondays and Wednesdays.
3 Many people _____ at home at least one day a week.
4 _____ you _____ for Matt? He's on his way now.
5 Most teenagers _____ a lot of time on their phones and computers every day.
6 _____ you _____ your laptop right now, or can I borrow it?

Question forms: *Do, did,* and *be* ▶1.2

3 Complete the questions with the correct form of *do* or *be*.

1 _____ you talk to your boss yesterday?
2 _____ Hugo at soccer practice last week?
3 _____ Japanese people smile more than North Americans?
4 _____ pointing rude in your culture?
5 Why _____ people frown?
6 What _____ you laugh at earlier?
7 _____ Briana and Mei good friends now?
8 Who _____ you see at the mall yesterday?

4 Complete the conversations. Use the correct form of *be* or *do* and *wh-* question words if needed.

1 A: _____ you greet people with a kiss?
   B: No, I don't. I'm from Canada.
2 A: _____ that woman over there?
   B: The one with dark hair? She's my sister.
3 A: _____ Irina talk about in class last night?
   B: She talked about emotions in animals.
4 A: _____ your parents surprised at the news?
   B: Yes, they were.
5 A: _____ people show enjoyment?
   B: Their eyes become narrow, and the corners of their mouths go up.
6 A: _____ Darwin write about emotions?
   B: Yes, he did.

Tag questions in the present tenses: *Be* and *do* ▶1.3

5 Match the statements with the correct tag questions.

1 You're friends with Han, ____   a isn't he?
2 He's working, ____   b do they?
3 They don't speak English, ____   c doesn't it?
4 The party starts soon, ____   d do we?
5 She isn't living in London, ____   e is she?
6 We don't have time, ____   f aren't you?

6 Complete the tag questions. Use the correct form of *be* or *do*.

1 Jack is one of your old friends, _____?
2 You don't know Lisa very well, _____?
3 She gets bored easily, _____?
4 Facial expressions tell us a lot, _____?
5 We're not leaving now, _____?
6 You and Rick work together, _____?
7 It isn't time to leave yet, _____?
8 Ken and Reiko are from Tokyo, _____?

Communication ▶1.1

1 Rewrite the questions using the correct forms of the phrases in the box.

deal with	have an influence on
keep in touch with	look forward to
look up to	work something out

1 Who do you admire?

_____

2 What affects your success at work or school?

_____

3 How do you manage difficult deadlines?

_____

4 How do you stay in contact with your family?

_____

5 What are you excited about?

_____

6 What kind of problems are easy to find solutions for?

_____

2 Answer the questions in Exercise 2 about yourself.

1 _____

2 _____

3 _____

4 _____

5 _____

6 _____

Body language and emotions ▶1.2

3 Match the definitions with the words.

1	a strong negative feeling	____	a	kiss
2	a state without strong feelings	____	b	point
3	move one's hand	____	c	wave
4	touch with one's lips	____	d	anger
5	pleasure, happiness	____	e	calm
6	direct attention with one's finger	____	f	enjoyment

4 Look at the photo. Check *Yes* or *No* to answer the questions.

		Yes	No
1	Is the grandmother kissing the baby?	☐	☐
2	Is the baby waving goodbye?	☐	☐
3	Are they pointing at something?	☐	☐
4	Does this activity bring them enjoyment?	☐	☐
5	Do they feel anger?	☐	☐
6	Does the baby feel calm?	☐	☐

VOCABULARY DEVELOPMENT: Adverbs of Manner ▶1.3

5 Complete the sentences with the words in the box.

calmly	fully	angrily	simply	gradually

1 Alex works well with difficult customers. He always answers them _____ and never raises his voice.

2 It's easier for me to learn vocabulary if I do it _____—just a few words at a time.

3 I don't _____ understand the process. Can you explain it to me?

4 I'm sorry that I answered _____. I was upset.

5 The office is designed very _____. There are a few tables and chairs, but it's mostly open space.

6 Complete the text. Change the adjectives in parentheses to adverbs.

When you travel to a new country, watch how people interact. Do they speak [1]_____ (loud) or [2]_____ (quiet)? Do they greet each other [3]_____ (calm) or [4]_____ (excited)? Do they shake hands [5]_____ (firm) or [6]_____ (gentle)? Or do they bow [7]_____ (deep) when they meet new people?

READING SKILL: Skimming ▶1.2

1 Skim the blog post. Complete the sentence.

The two main kinds of communication are _____ and _____.

Ⓠℝ Talking with Words

That title sounds like I'm repeating myself, doesn't it? Of course, we talk with words, don't we? Well, linguists, the scientists who study language, might disagree. They are interested in both verbal and nonverbal forms of communication.

What is verbal communication?

It's when we use words to communicate. There are different ways to send and receive information with words. To understand information fully, the sender and receiver need to know the same language.

- Verbal input: listening and reading comprehension
- Verbal output: speaking and writing

What is nonverbal communication?

It's when we "talk" without words.

- Nonverbal input: hearing sounds and seeing objects and movements. For example, when someone laughs or hits the table angrily, they are definitely telling us something about their feelings of enjoyment or anger, aren't they?
- Nonverbal output: making facial expressions like smiling, using gestures like waving, and performing actions like turning and walking away.

How do we use different kinds of communication?

There are many combinations of ways to receive and send information. For ordinary conversation, the most important combination is speaking ↔ listening comprehension.

Linguists study such combinations to understand communication. For example, to follow instructions, you need to understand the words you hear or read, and then use action in response. To point at a named object, you need to see the object and understand the word.

—Adapted from *The Oxford Companion to Medicine*, 3rd ed. by Stephen Lock, John M. Last, and George Dunea

2 Skim the blog post again. Choose the three main ideas.

- ☐ The title repeats ideas.
- ☐ Linguists might disagree with the writer of the blog post.
- ☐ Verbal communication includes listening, speaking, reading, and writing.
- ☐ Nonverbal communication includes sounds, things we see, gestures, and actions.
- ☐ Turning and walking away is an action.
- ☐ You need to understand words to follow instructions.
- ☐ We use more than one way to communicate.

3 Choose the correct answers to the questions.

1 Which of these is NOT a way the writer shows important information?
   a Titles and section headings
   b Bullets
   c Italics
   d Questions

2 How many main sections are in the blog post?
   a 1   b 2
   c 3   d 4

READING: Practice

4 Read the blog post. Complete the sentences.

1 Linguists are scientists who study _____.

2 When we use words to communicate, we are using _____ communication.

3 The sender and receiver of information need to know _____.

4 When we use nonverbal communication, we talk without _____.

5 Information we take in is _____.

6 Information we send to other people is _____.

7 Linguists study _____ to understand how we communicate.

8 For ordinary conversation, the most important ways to communicate are
_____ and _____.

5 Match the ideas from the blog post with the examples.

_____ 1 verbal input   a writing

_____ 2 verbal output   b walking away

_____ 3 nonverbal input   c reading

_____ 4 facial expression   d waving

_____ 5 gesture   e smile

_____ 6 action   f understands words, acts in response

_____ 7 following instructions   g sounds

6 Complete the chart with details from the blog post.

Communication			
Verbal		1 _____ Nonverbal _____	
2 _____	output	input	3 _____
listening 6 _____	4 _____ writing	5 _____ 7 _____	making facial expressions using gestures 8 _____

1 Complete the conversation from Scene 1 of the video with the words in the box.

going	Hey	How	later	see	what's

Max: Hey, Andy! You're back!

Andy: [1]_____, Max. What's [2]_____?

Max: Hello, Kevin! So, how's it [3]_____? [4]_____ was your vacation?

Kevin: Great, thanks! Well, I gotta go to the bookstore. I'll catch up with you [5]_____!

Max: OK, [6]_____ you!

2 Complete the conversation from Scene 2 of the video with the words in the box.

We're fine	Hello	Have a good weekend	How are you
Nice to see you	Take care	Good afternoon	

Prof. Lopez: Max! Andy! [1]_____!

Max: [2]_____, Professor Lopez.

Andy: [3]_____?

Prof. Lopez: Oh, I have a little bit of a cold. Achoo! Excuse me. How are you both?

Max: Uh … .[4]_____, thanks!

Andy: Yes. Glad to be back! Ready for the new semester!

Prof. Lopez: Oh, excellent. Well, I'm going to a faculty meeting. [5]_____!

Max: Thanks, you too! [6]_____.

Andy: [7]_____!

3 Read the conversation. Then choose the correct words to complete the sentences.

Karen: Hey, Ann. What's up?

Ann: Good afternoon, Karen. How are you?

Karen: Great, thanks! Oh my, it's late. I have to meet someone. I'll catch up with you later.

Ann: It's nice to see you. I want to talk to you about something.

Karen: Sounds good, but I have to go now.

1 Karen *is / isn't* very formal.

2 The speakers *know / don't know* each other.

3 Ann *is / isn't* more formal than Karen.

4 Both speakers *greet each other / have meetings*.

5 Karen *wants / doesn't want* to have a long conversation.

6 *Karen / Ann* ends the conversation.

4 Rewrite Ann's lines to make them them more appropriate.

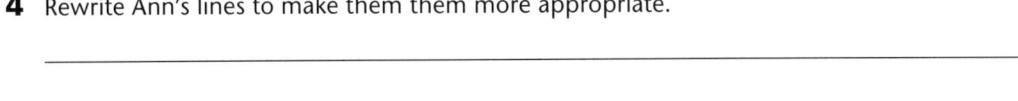

UNIT REVIEW: Podcast

GO ONLINE to listen to the podcast from the Unit Review.

1 Listen to the Unit Review Podcast. Are the statements True, False, or Not Given?

	True	False	Not Given
1 The woman is a psychologist.	☐	☐	☐
2 They're talking about many kinds of relationships.	☐	☐	☐
3 Friends actually feel the same thing emotionally.	☐	☐	☐
4 Most of us can tell who our real friends are.	☐	☐	☐
5 Women make better friends than men.	☐	☐	☐

2 Listen to the podcast again. Choose the correct words to complete the sentences.

1 True friends _____ each other.

   a have a great influence on   b lend money to   c tell secrets to

2 The psychologist says friends are often _____ each other.

   a similar to   b different from   c exactly the same as

3 Our _____ change as a result of friendship.

   a goals   b brains   c bodies

4 We get _____ friendships as we get older.

   a better at   b more interested in   c less comfortable with

LISTENING SKILL: Guessing meaning from context ▶ 1.1

3 Listen to the sentences from the podcast. What part of speech are the underlined words? Write *N* (noun), *V* (verb), *Adj* (adjective), or *Adv* (adverb) on the lines.

1 Good friendships last a lifetime. _____

2 Even our brains change as a result of an ongoing friendship. _____

3 Because we experience the same thing emotionally, we want to help each other. _____

4 That's a good indication of a real friendship. _____

5 A study of friendships showed that we're actually bad at judging who our genuine friends are. _____

4 Write the words from Exercise 3 next to the correct definitions.

1 sign _____   4 real _____

2 the length of a life _____   5 in a manner that shows _____

3 continuing _____   great feeling

DISCUSSION BOARD PREPARATION

5 Look at the Unit 1 Review Discussion Point. Read the questions in the prompt. Then read the reply. How many ways does the writer mention she tries to be a friend?

_____

6 Label the parts of the reply that answer the three questions from the prompt.

_____

Unit 1 Review Discussion Point

1 Read the quote. In what ways do you try to be a friend?
"The only way to have a friend is to be one."
—Ralph Waldo Emerson, selected from *Oxford Essential Quotations*, 5th ed., edited by Susan Ratcliffe
2 Is there anything you wouldn't do for a friend?
3 How do you think friendships change over your life?

Latest: Ifemelu
two hours ago
I try to be a friend in several ways. First, I listen to my friends when they are dealing with problems. Sometimes I help them work out solutions. Second, I simply make time for them. Even when I'm busy, I keep in touch by phone or email. I look forward to the time we spend together, and try to show I appreciate them. I also try to encourage my friends to follow their dreams.

While I always try to help my friends, I wouldn't do anything I thought was wrong, like lie or steal. Good friends don't ask you to do something wrong. In fact, I think good friends encourage you to be the best person you can be.

Friendships change as we grow older because we need different things at different times. When you're a child or a teenager, a friend is someone to do fun things with. When you're a little older, a friend gives good advice. When you're much older, a friend can help you remember good times. Friendships change over your life because you are gradually changing, too.

7 Overall, did the writer answer all the questions? If yes, explain. If no, what can the writer change? Then use the rubric to give a score for the reply. Give points: 0 (not successful)– 10 (successful).

Writing a Discussion Board Post	Points
The post answers the questions clearly and completely.	
The post has a general opening sentence and a general closing sentence.	
The post uses grammar and vocabulary from the unit.	
The post shows careful thinking about the topic.	
Sentences are complete and have correct punctuation.	
The post is long enough (180–220 words).	
Total	

WRITE YOUR POST

8 Read the quote. In what ways do you try to be a friend? Is there anything you wouldn't do for a friend? How do you think friendships change over your life? Write a draft of your post for the Unit 1 Review Discussion Board.

"The only way to have a friend is to be one."
—Ralph Waldo Emerson, selected from *Oxford Essential Quotations*,
5th ed., edited by Susan Ratcliffe

9 Use the rubric from Exercise 7 to score your post. Then improve your post.

 Go ONLINE to add your comments to the discussion board.

2 Time

Simple past: *Be* ▶2.1

1 Choose the correct words to complete the sentences.

1 There *was / were* a lot of people at the concert.
2 The musicians *was / were* really good.
3 The traffic *was / were* terrible, and everyone *was / were* annoyed.
4 It *was / were* late when we got home.
5 I *wasn't / weren't* able to fall asleep right away.
6 It *was / were* the first big event in the new stadium.

2 Rewrite the sentences in simple past.

1 There aren't any tall buildings in the town.

_____

2 The lake is very close to my house.

_____

3 There's a park in the neighborhood.

_____

4 Most of my neighbors are really friendly.

_____

5 I'm not old enough to drive to school.

_____

Simple past and past continuous ▶2.2

3 Match the sentences with the correct uses of the past tense verb.

___ 1 My parents lived in Milan.
___ 2 At midnight I was still studying.
___ 3 The wind was blowing hard.
___ 4 We played soccer every afternoon.
___ 5 She got dressed and then ate breakfast.
___ 6 They were crossing the street when the accident happened.

a order of events
b repeated action
c past state
d action in progress
e describing a scene
f shorter action interrupting longer action

4 Choose the correct words to complete the sentences.

1 At eight o'clock last night we *studied / were studying* at the library.
2 She *sent / was sending* the email yesterday.
3 The factory *closed / was closing* in 1973.
4 While we *watched / were watching* the movie, the power *went / was going* off.
5 Everything *was / was being* a little crazy during the fire. All around me, people *pushed / were pushing* to get outside quickly.
6 Over several weeks, the researchers *showed / were showing* photos to the participants in the study.

Used to ▶2.3

5 Complete the sentences. Use *used to* or *didn't use to* and the verbs in parentheses.

1 In the 1960s, Detroit _____ (be) a busy city.
2 The Detroit auto industry _____ (make) most of the cars in the United States.
3 Many people _____ (work) downtown.
4 At that time, the downtown area _____ (not, have) abandoned and empty buildings.
5 Businesses _____ (provide) many job opportunities.
6 People _____ (not, dress) as casually as some people do now.

6 Read about Ava's life now. Then write sentences about how Ava's life has changed. Use *used to* or *didn't use to* and any words in parentheses.

1 Ava is happy. (sad)

_____

2 She has many friends.

_____

3 Her family lives in the city. (countryside)

_____

4 She has a lot of things to do on weekends.

_____

5 She doesn't walk to school.

_____

Changing times ▶2.1

1 Choose the correct words to complete the sentences.

1 The population showed *growth / a decrease* over time, falling from 300,000 to 150,000.

2 The auto industry didn't begin to *replace / recover* for a long time. Now it's doing better.

3 A few decades ago, people left the town, but that trend has begun to *abandon / reverse*. Now people are moving back.

4 When people *abandon / recover* neighborhoods, the empty buildings are often unsafe.

5 One *decrease / benefit* of people moving back to a city is new construction.

6 Solar energy is beginning to *recover / replace* coal and oil in many communities.

7 This shift to solar has led to a *benefit / decline* of the coal industry.

8 Many people are moving to Suzhou, China. Its rate of *growth / decline* is almost 6% a year.

2 Choose the correct answers to the questions.

1 What is an example of a city's growth?
   a The number of businesses increase.
   b Businesses abandon the downtown area.

2 What is a benefit of more companies coming to a region?
   a Traffic or pollution may increase.
   b There may be more jobs.

3 What might cause a city to begin to decline?
   a There's a rise in crime.
   b There's a growth in job opportunities.

4 Which is a better place for a young family to live?
   a a city with an increase in noise problems
   b a town with a rise in the quality of schools

5 What change is a sign that a neighborhood is improving?
   a a decrease in the number of people moving in
   b more small businesses are recovering

6 How can cities reverse a rise in crime?
   a with an increase in community police
   b with a decrease in lighting

VOCABULARY DEVELOPMENT: Phrases with time ▶2.2

3 Choose the correct words to complete the sentences.

1 We missed the flight. We didn't get to the gate _____ time.
   a long   b in   c spend

2 The _____ time I went to Japan, I lost my wallet.
   a first   b through   c have

3 Are you always _____ time, or are you sometimes late?
   a this   b on   c make

4 Don't _____ your time complaining.
   a next   b in   c waste

5 Traffic has improved _____ time.
   a that   b over   c run out of

6 She can't remember the _____ time she was there.
   a last   b over   c spend

4 Complete the sentences with the words in the box.

the next	a long	that	run out of
over	make	have	spend

1 We'll bring swimsuits _____ time we visit.

2 I hope I finish the test. I often _____ time and don't answer everything.

3 The meeting took _____ time, so they were late.

4 She didn't like her apartment building at first, but she began to appreciate it _____ time.

5 Do you _____ a lot of time with your family?

6 At his last job, he didn't _____ any time to relax.

7 Do you remember _____ time we went to Mexico?

8 People need to _____ time for family and friends.

READING SKILL: Scanning ▶2.2

1 Scan the article. Complete the sentence.

The article is about _____.

Circadian Rhythms: Morning Lark or Night Owl?

The time of day affects how we feel because of circadian rhythms—body changes that happen every 24 hours.

Circadian rhythms include changes in body temperature, heart rate, and strength, which affect many physical activities. For example, there's a decrease in our body temperature overnight, but it recovers gradually throughout the day. Several studies

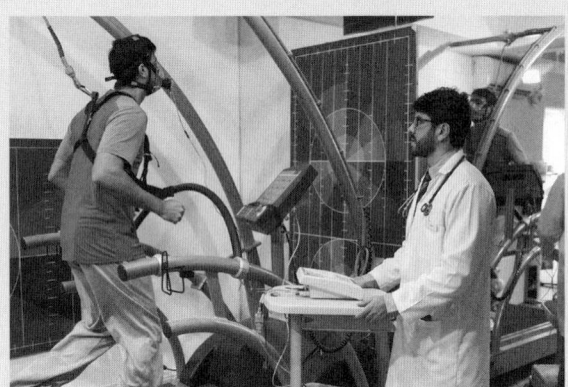

showed that runners, cyclists, and swimmers did best in between 4:30–5:30 p.m., especially for activities that lasted a short time. Those results were probably a benefit of warmer muscles. However, fencers performed better midday, perhaps because their sport demands mental skills, which decline after noon. The time of day made a difference for some athletes who were attempting to break records.

Researchers used to think people had similar circadian rhythms, but recent studies showed personality and environment affect someone's body clock. Shy people often function better in the morning, while outgoing people are better later in the day. And, in 2015, a study showed that people who liked to wake up early and work in the morning performed better early in the day than those who liked to wake up later and work in the evenings.

U.S. scientists Jeffrey Hall, Michael Rosbash, and Michael Young won the 2017 Nobel Prize for physiology or medicine for their important research on circadian rhythms.

—Adapted from *Food and Fitness: A Dictionary of Diet and Exercise*, 2nd ed. by Michael Kent

2 Scan the article. Choose the correct answers to the questions.

1 How often do circadian rhythms happen?
   a every 12 hours
   b every 24 hours
   c every 36 hours

2 According to the article, what three physical changes are due to circadian rhythms?
   a body temperature, heart rate, and strength
   b blood pressure, strength, and breathing
   c amount of sleep, energy, and heart rate

3 When do runners perform best?
   a 8:30–9:30 a.m.
   b noon–2:00 p.m.
   c 4:30–5:30 p.m.

4 When was the study that showed people who like to wake up early do better in the morning?
   a 2010   b 2012   c 2015

5 What year did the researchers win the Nobel Prize?
   a 1999   b 2015   c 2017

3 Scan the article again. Match the beginnings of the phrases in A with the endings in B.

A

1 morning lark or

2 body temperature, heart rate, and

3 runners, cyclists, and

4 personality and

5 Jeffrey Hall, Michael Rosbach, and

6 physiology or

B

_____ a strength

_____ b Michael Young

_____ c environment

_____ d medicine

_____ e swimmers

_____ f night owl

READING: Practice

4 Read the article in Activity 1. Choose the sentence that is the best statement of the main idea.

☐ Athletes do better with warm muscles.

☐ Some people like to do things in the morning.

☐ Circadian rhythms affect how well people perform, including in sports.

☐ Three scientists won a Nobel prize for their work on circadian rhythms.

5 Read the article again. Are the statements True, False or Not Given?

		True	False	Not Given
1	Circadian rhythms happen over a week.	☐	☐	☐
2	Our body temperature changes over the course of the day.	☐	☐	☐
3	Strength is not affected by the time of day.	☐	☐	☐
4	Our body temperature drops rapidly when we fall asleep.	☐	☐	☐
5	Runners are faster in the morning.	☐	☐	☐
6	Warmer muscles probably help athletes perform better.	☐	☐	☐
7	Fencers need to think in their sport.	☐	☐	☐
8	Outgoing people do better around 3:00 p.m.	☐	☐	☐
9	People who like to wake up early are better at sports.	☐	☐	☐
10	Circadian rhythms are not an important area of research.	☐	☐	☐

6 Complete the chart with details from the article.

outgoing person	swimmer	runner	shy person	cyclist	fencer
person who likes to wake up late		person who likes to wake up early			

Does better earlier in the day	Does better later in the day

REAL-WORLD ENGLISH: Apologizing ▶2.4

1 Complete the conversation from Scene 1 of the video with the words in the box.

is it	I thought	on my way	reading	Sorry	Where

Max: Andy?

Andy: Hey, Max.

Max: ^{1}_____ are you?

Kevin: Huh? What time ^{2}_____?

Max: It's six-thirty! We're all here for the English Lit study group. ^{3}_____ you were coming!

Andy: Oh, no…I'm late. Sorry, I was ^{4}_____ and…^{5}_____, Max! I'm ^{6}_____!

2 Complete the conversation from Scene 2 of the video with the words in the box.

let me help	my fault	OK	wasn't watching	so sorry

Prof. Jackson: Look out!

Andy: Oh, no. Professor Jackson! I'm ^{1}_____. It was completely ^{2}_____.

Prof. Jackson: It's ^{3}_____. I was texting, and I ^{4}_____ where I was going.

Andy: I'm late for a meeting, so I was in a hurry. Here, ^{5}_____ you.

3 Match the functions with the sentences.

____ 1   Say you're sorry   a   Let me help you clean it up.

____ 2   Give an explanation   b   I completely forgot.

____ 3   Take responsibility   c   It's my fault.

____ 4   Promise to do better   d   I'm really, really sorry.

____ 5   Offer to fix the problem   e   It won't happen again.

4 Put the following conversation in order.

____ OK. I guess that'll work.

____ I know. I can take you tomorrow.

____ Thanks for understanding. I promise it won't happen again.

____ Why do we have to leave now? You said we could stay until 5:00.

____ But we'll miss the show.

____ I'm really sorry. It's my fault. I forgot I have homework due tomorrow.

5 Answer the questions about the conversation in Exercise 4.

1   Do the speakers know each other? How do you know?

_____

2   Why is the first speaker upset?

_____

3   What explanation does the second speaker give? How does she offer to fix the problem?

_____

LISTENING SKILL: Previewing ▶2.1

1 Look at the podcast photo. What do you think the podcast will say? Check your predictions.

☐ Paying attention to your breathing is a good way to focus on the present.

☐ The things you pay attention to can affect how fast time passes.

☐ Things like meditation and yoga make time go faster.

☐ It takes a lot of time to practice meditation.

☐ Closing your eyes is a great way to pay attention to your thoughts.

☐ Men should meditate more.

☐ Listening to stories makes time pass more slowly.

Mind What You Say

Episode 4:
Your mind and time

UNIT REVIEW: Podcast

🔘 **GO ONLINE to listen to the podcast from the Unit Review.**

2 🔊 Listen to the Unit Review Podcast. Write the statements from Exercise 1 that were correct.

1 _____

2 _____

3 🔊 Listen to the podcast again. Choose the correct words to complete the sentences.

1 The podcast is about _____.

a your mind b your body c both your mind and your body

2 Kevin Jameson writes about _____.

a mindfulness b yoga c time

3 When you are mindful, you _____.

a exercise b pay attention c study a lot

4 _____ is NOT a benefit of mindfulness.

a an increase in anxiety b an increase in focus c a slowing down of time

5 In the study, people who listened to a mindfulness exercise thought time lasted _____.

a shorter b the same amount of time c longer

DISCUSSION BOARD PREPARATION

4 Look at the Unit 2 Review Discussion Point. Read the questions in the prompt. Then read the reply. What example does the writer give to explain how time passed when she was a child?

_____

5 Why does the writer mention technology?

_____

6 What is the writer trying to say in the last sentence of the post?

_____

Unit 2 Review Discussion Point

1 Read the quote. Do you think our lives get busier as time goes on?
   "Nobody sees a flower—really—it is so small—we haven't time—and to see takes time."
   —Georgia O'Keeffe, selected from *The Oxford Dictionary of American Quotations*, 2nd ed.,
   edited by Hugh Rawson and Margaret Miner
2 How is your life busier now than in the past?
3 Do you feel like time moves too fast? If so, how can you slow it down?

Latest: **Maria**
three hours ago
I do feel like life gets busier as time goes by. When I was a child, time used to move slowly, but over time it sped up. A school day used to feel like it lasted forever. When I was studying at the university, I only had to think about myself and my classes. I felt busy, but I still had time to do the things I enjoyed.

Now time moves very fast, maybe too fast. My life is very busy with my job and my family. I work Monday through Friday and then come home and take care of my family and do household chores. On the weekends, I have to do laundry and go grocery shopping. It's hard to relax. Technology also makes me feel very busy and takes up too much time.

When I feel like time is moving too fast, I turn off my TV and phone to try to slow things down. I spend more time with my family and friends. I focus on the present instead of the past or future, and that helps slow time down. I think we need to pay attention to our lives before we run out of time.

7 Overall, did the writer answer all the questions? If yes, explain. If no, what can the writer change? Then use the rubric to give a score for the reply. Give points: 0 (not successful)–10 (successful).

_____

_____

Writing a Discussion Board Post	Points
The post answers the questions clearly and completely.	
The post has a general opening sentence and a general closing sentence.	
The post uses grammar and vocabulary from the unit.	
The post shows careful thinking about the topic.	
Sentences are complete and have correct punctuation.	
The post is long enough (180–220 words).	
Total	

WRITE YOUR POST

8 Read the quote. Do you think our lives get busier as time goes on? How is your life busier now than in the past? Do you feel like time moves too fast? What do you do to slow it down? Write a draft of your post for the Unit 2 Review Discussion Board.

   *"Nobody sees a flower—really—it is so small—we haven't time—and to see takes time."*
—Georgia O'Keeffe, selected from *The Oxford Dictionary of American Quotations*, 2nd ed., edited by Hugh Rawson and Margaret Miner

9 Use the rubric from Exercise 7 to score your post. Then improve your post.

  GO ONLINE to add your comments to the discussion board.

3 Learning

Present perfect simple with *for* and *since* ▶3.1

1 Complete the sentences with *for* or *since*.

1 Keiko has studied English _____ 2005.

2 We've lived in Oman _____ eight months.

3 Our sales have increased _____ six years.

4 The company has hired dozens of new employees _____ last spring.

5 How often have you changed jobs _____ you worked here?

2 Answer the questions in complete sentences using the words in parentheses.

1 How long have you lived in London? (three years)

_____

2 How long has your sister worked there? (2012)

_____

3 How long has Thien wanted to be a chef? (a year)

_____

4 How long have they had your application? (Monday)

_____

5 How long has the job opening been on the website? (two weeks)

_____

Present perfect and simple past ▶3.2

3 Complete the sentences using the correct forms of the verbs in parentheses.

1 Three people _____ against the robot so far. (play)

2 I _____ putting the robot together yesterday. (finish)

3 Technology _____ some jobs away from people in recent years. (take)

4 However, last year technology _____ thousands of new jobs. (provide)

5 He _____ the first robot, but he _____ many in the last few years. (not, invent; build)

4 Complete the text with verbs in the box. Use the simple past or present perfect.

be	begin	change	deliver
research	stay	use	

Technology ^{1}_____ jobs in many fields, including healthcare. Last year I ^{2}_____ in a hospital. The hospital ^{3}_____ a fleet of robots that ^{4}_____ medicine and meals. Since then, I ^{5}_____ the topic of robots in healthcare. The human workers ^{6}_____ to appreciate their robot co-workers.

Present perfect with *just, already, yet, ever, never,* and *still* ▶3.3

5 Match the adverbs with their uses.

____ 1 never ____ 3 still ____ 5 ever

____ 2 yet ____ 4 just ____ 6 already

a used in negative sentences to talk about actions that we expected to happen before now

b used in negative sentences and questions to talk about actions we expect to happen

c used in positive sentences to talk about recent news

d used in positive sentences to talk about events that happened before now or earlier than expected

e used in questions to mean "at any time in the past"

f used to mean "at no time in the past"

6 Complete the sentences with the correct adverbs from Exercise 5.

1 I've _____ taken a course online, but I want to next semester.

2 My instructor _____ hasn't provided online resources, although we've asked her to.

3 She hasn't heard about her application _____, but she should hear very soon.

4 Why am I so happy? I've _____ found out that I passed the course!

5 Have you _____ thought about graduate programs?

6 He's _____ taken the course, but it was a few years ago.

VOCABULARY DEVELOPMENT:
Verbs and nouns from adjectives ▶3.1

1 Write the noun form or verb form of the adjectives.

1 confident (noun) _____

2 responsible (noun) _____

3 kind (noun) _____

4 valuable (verb) _____

5 understanding (verb) _____

6 acceptable (verb) _____

7 active (verb) _____

2 Complete the sentences with the noun or verb forms of the underlined words.

1 Kyori is very creative. She _____ interesting art projects out of recycled materials.

2 Adnan is one of our most reliable employees. We can _____ on him to complete his tasks on time.

3 Please let us know when you are available to practice. Respond with your _____.

4 I'm not sure that's a suitable position for him. Working with children might _____ him better.

5 We're very committed to this project. How can we show you our _____?

Verbs to describe robots ▶3.2

3 Choose the correct meaning of the word in **bold**.

1 The company **announced** the sale of a new smart phone.
   a made a formal public statement
   b made known the arrival of a guest

2 They will **perform** the operation in the morning.
   a present to an audience
   b carry out

3 I'm terrible with faces. I often don't **recognize** people.
   a accept the existence of something
   b identify someone or something

4 She just **realized** that Joe is the new teacher.
   a became aware
   b achieved

5 He **refuses** to talk to a robot.
   a does not allow someone to do something
   b is not willing to do something

6 Can you **solve** this math problem?
   a give an explanation for
   b find an answer to

4 Complete the text with the correct forms of the verbs from Exercise 3.

Several large automakers have [1]_____ that they will make driverless cars. However, carmakers will have to [2]_____ some problems first. For example, driverless cars need to [3]_____ traffic signs, emergency vehicles, and maybe even your own face. If the car knows who you are, it can [4]_____ certain adjustments, such as moving the seat. Some people still [5]_____ to ride in a driverless car because they worry about safety. That's because people often don't [6]_____ how safe these cars are!

Taking a course ▶3.3

5 Match the definitions with words from the box.

attend	certificate	degree	educate
essay	presentation	register	

1 an official document _____

2 an academic level _____

3 a short piece of writing _____

4 a speech or talk _____

5 go to a school, class _____

6 enter a list, sign up for _____

7 instruct, teach _____

6 Complete the sentences with the correct words from the box in Exercise 5.

1 Classes start soon, so we need to _____ today.

2 When we finish the course, we'll get a _____.

3 My _____ is in biology, but I want to go to graduate school in computer engineering.

4 Did you read this _____ on distance learning?

5 They're giving a _____ on the benefits of online learning.

6 Governments have a responsibility to _____ all their citizens by providing good schools.

7 What school did you _____ as a child?

1 Read the article. Complete the sentence with the correct information.

The animals mentioned in the article include _____.

Learning in Animals

An animal is more likely to survive if it changes its behavior because of experience. Learning helps it get food, recognize danger, and solve problems in its environment. Experimental psychologists have been interested in animal learning since the early twentieth century. Scientists studying animals under laboratory conditions realized the importance of learning in the development of behavior. These researchers have demonstrated how rats could be trained, or "conditioned," by giving them food rewards or harming them with electric shocks. Others have criticized this work, especially those who observe animals in their natural surroundings and who stress the importance of biology in behavioral development. More recently scientists have accepted a combination of these approaches: learning is necessary to an animal's development, occurring in response to the animal's environment but within limits set by the animal's biology.

Scientists have identified several ways animals learn. In conditioning, animals learn to associate one thing with another. For example, a bird learns that an orange and black caterpillar has a bad taste. Trial-and-error learning happens when an animal's actions accidentally produces a reward, such as food. The animal then repeats the behavior to get the reward. Some animals, like chimpanzees, use insight learning, meaning they perform behaviors to solve problems. For example, they can stack crates to reach bananas that are too high.

—Adapted from *A Dictionary of Biology*, 7th ed. edited by Robert Hine and Elizabeth Martin

2 Read the article again. Complete the summary paragraph with the words in the box.

biology	conditioning	insight	laboratory
learn	response	surroundings	trial-and-error

Animals are more likely to survive if they ¹_____ from experience. Scientists have studied

animals in the ²_____ and in their natural ³_____. They believe animal learning

is a ⁴_____ to the environment within limits set by the animal's ⁵_____. Three ways

that animals learn are: ⁶_____ (associating one thing with another), ⁷_____ (learning

accidentally), and ⁸_____ (problem-solving).

3 Read the statements. Are the statements True, False, or Not Given?

		True	False	Not Given
1	The ability to learn helps animals survive.	☐	☐	☐
2	Only a few animals can learn.	☐	☐	☐
3	Early researchers studied animals in laboratories.	☐	☐	☐
4	They didn't try to train the animals, they only observed them.	☐	☐	☐
5	Rats learn to escape from their cages.	☐	☐	☐
6	Scientists think learning is mostly biological.	☐	☐	☐
7	Animals can learn to associate color with taste.	☐	☐	☐
8	Animals repeat something that is rewarding.	☐	☐	☐
9	Chimpanzees can solve problems.	☐	☐	☐

REAL-WORLD READING

4 Complete the sentences with the correct information from the article.

1 Learning helps animals to survive by helping them get food, _____,

and _____.

2 Scientists began to study animal learning in the early _____.

3 One way they trained rats was by harming them with _____.

4 Although some researchers study animals in laboratories, others study them in their

_____.

5 Conditioning is learning to _____ one thing with another.

6 When an animal produces a reward accidentally, it learns through

_____ learning.

7 A chimpanzee can stack crates to reach _____.

READING SKILL: Recognizing and understanding synonyms ▶3.4

5 Match the words and phrases from the article with their synonyms.

____	1 researchers	a	environment
____	2 train	b	problem-solving
____	3 surroundings	c	scientists
____	4 observe	d	study, watch
____	5 behavior	e	condition
____	6 insight learning	f	actions

6 Write synonyms from the article for the words below.

1 live _____

2 show _____

3 hurting _____

4 determined _____

5 growth _____

6 mixture _____

7 needed _____

8 connect _____

9 something good _____

REAL-WORLD ENGLISH: Getting clarification ▶ 3.4

1 Put the two conversations from the video in order.

A

____ Ah, I see. Thank you.

____ So...for Monday, please read pages 416–452 in your Art History books. Have a good weekend.

____ Um...pages 416–452.

____ Sorry, so I didn't quite catch what pages?

B

____ Sorry? What did you say?

____ Oh, got it.

____ What pages did she tell us to read? 460 to...?

____ Uh, no. Four sixteen...to four fifty-two.

____ Hey! What was that about the reading?

2 Match the beginnings of the expressions with the endings.

1	Could you	____	a	quite catch that.
2	Can you go	____	b	repeat that, please?
3	Sorry, I didn't	____	c	explaining that?
4	Sorry, I'm	____	d	over that again?
5	Do you mind	____	e	not sure I understand.
6	What	____	f	do you mean?

3 Read the conversation, and find the expressions for clarifying.

Interviewer: Could you please tell me more about your background in marketing?
Applicant: Sure. I worked on a campaign at my university to market a MOOC.
Interviewer: Sorry, I didn't quite catch that. To market what?
Applicant: A MOOC.
Interviewer: What exactly does that mean? Massive Open Online Course?
Applicant: Huh?
Interviewer: Does *MOOC* mean "Massive Open Online Course"?
Applicant: Yeah, that's right. And we marketed it mostly through social media.

4 Answer the questions about the conversation in Exercise 3.

1 Do the speakers know each other? How do you know that?

_____

2 Which speaker is more formal? What expressions show that?

_____

3 Do you think the applicant is a strong candidate for the job? Why or why not?

_____

4 Do the speakers make any mistakes? If so, what are they?

_____

UNIT REVIEW: Podcast

GO ONLINE to listen to the podcast from the Unit Review.

1 Listen to the Unit Review Podcast. What kind of learning are they discussing?

2 Listen to the podcast again. Complete the sentences with the words in the box.

certificate	game designer	high school	internship
knowledge	responsibilities	universities	

1   Sunju has worked at several _____.

2   Her daughter is in _____ and has gotten a(n) _____ in coding online.

3   Now her daughter is doing a(n) _____ with a video game design company.

4   She has a lot of _____ and performs the duties of a(n) _____.

5   This kind of learning recognizes that everyone brings _____ to a learning situation.

3 Listen to the podcast again. Are the statements True, False, or Not Given?

		True	False	Not Given
1	The host knew the guest well before the podcast recording.	☐	☐	☐
2	Experiential learning takes place outside the classroom.	☐	☐	☐
3	Learning to cook is an example of traditional learning.	☐	☐	☐
4	Sunju's daughter wants to make phone apps.	☐	☐	☐
5	Sunju's daughter wants to get a degree in coding.	☐	☐	☐

LISTENING SKILL: Understanding a speaker's purpose   ▶ 3.3

4 Listen to the sections from the podcast, and write *P* (persuade), *I* (inform), or *E* (entertain) to identify the purpose.

_____   1   You don't want to miss today's episode with Sunju Lee.

_____   2   She's a psychologist who's also worked in administration at several universities.

_____   3   Basically, experiential learning takes place outside a traditional classroom…
The learner doesn't attend class, but instead is involved in a meaningful experience.

_____   4   So, this hands-on experience is not about avoiding class?

_____   5   If more schools realized the value of experience in learning, our educational systems would improve.

_____   6   I've always wanted to study Spanish, but maybe I'll go to Costa Rica for a few months instead of taking a class. Maybe they combine surfing with Spanish…

DISCUSSION BOARD PREPARATION

5 Look at the Unit 3 Review Discussion Point. Read the questions in the prompt. Then read the reply. What does the writer think happens when people learn?

_____

6 Label the parts of the reply that answer the three questions from the prompt.

_____

Unit 3 Review Discussion Point

1 Read the quote. Do you agree that learning and education are the best ways to change the world?
   "Education is the most powerful weapon which you can use to change the world."
   —Nelson Mandela, selected from *Oxford Essential Quotations*, 5th ed., edited by Susan Ratcliffe
2 In what ways do learning and education change the world?
3 What kind of learning or education works best?

Latest: **Azita**
two hours
I agree with Nelson Mandela. I think the best way to change the world is through learning and education. When people learn, they get more power. They understand how things work and what they can do. When people are educated, they can change the world because they start new businesses, invent new machines, and solve problems. Education is about sharing knowledge. When we know more, we can do more. In addition, we can teach others what we know. Sharing knowledge helps everyone. It can help people have better lives.

In my opinion, a combination of learning styles works best. I've learned a lot from excellent teachers. They have explained things that I didn't understand and given me confidence. I've also learned a lot from my own experience. I've been able to solve problems by myself because of what I've learned. I think that both classroom learning and experiential learning are very helpful. In addition, I think we can learn from online sources. I do a lot of reading on different websites, and I also take online classes sometimes. Although I like to be with other people when I learn, I realize I can also learn a lot online by myself.

7 Overall, did the writer answer all the questions? If yes, explain. If no, what can the writer change? Then use the rubric to give a score for the reply. Give points: 0 (not successful)–10 (successful).

Writing a Discussion Board Post	Points
The post answers the questions clearly and completely.	
The post has a general opening sentence and a general closing sentence.	
The post uses grammar and vocabulary from the unit.	
The post shows careful thinking about the topic.	
Sentences are complete and have correct punctuation.	
The post is long enough (180–220 words).	
Total	

WRITE YOUR POST

8 Read the quote. Do you agree that learning and education are the best ways to change the world? In what ways do learning and education change the world? What kind of learning or education works best? Write a draft of your post for the Unit 3 Review Discussion Board.

"Education is the most powerful weapon which you can use to change the world."
—Nelson Mandela, selected from *Oxford Essential Quotations*, 5th ed., edited by Susan Ratcliffe

9 Use the rubric from Exercise 7 to score your post. Then improve your post.

 Go ONLINE to add your comments to the discussion board.

4 Movement

Will vs. going to ▶4.1

1 Choose the correct words to complete the sentences.

1 Flavio *will* / *is going to* run in the race tomorrow.
2 That's a great idea! *We'll* / *We're going to* meet you at the gym.
3 The gym *will* / *is going to* add two new weight-lifting classes in January.
4 Cycling is great exercise. *You'll* / *You're going to* get in good shape quickly, I think.
5 The community center *will* / *is going to* show a film about parkour next week.
6 She *won't* / *isn't going to* be as tired from the workouts in a few weeks.

2 Write the words in the correct order to make sentences.

1 on / we're / soccer / to play / going / Saturday

   _____.

2 will / at the gym / they / how long / be

   _____?

3 to / you / going / where / are / hike

   _____?

4 after practice / home / won't / I / until / be

   _____.

5 that way / get / she / in shape / going to / isn't

   _____.

6 the / I / team / win / other / think / will

   _____.

Simple present in future time clauses ▶4.2

3 Complete the sentences. Use the verb in parentheses in simple present or with *will*.

1 When he _____ (arrive) in Thailand, he _____ (take) a bus to the mountains.
2 I _____ (call) as soon as I _____ (get) back from my trip.
3 The cruise ship _____ (visit) three islands before it _____ (return) to Miami.

4 After we _____ (see) the Eiffel Tower, we _____ (eat) lunch.
5 When it _____ (stop) raining, they _____ (open) the water park again.
6 Alana _____ (look) for a job if she _____ (come) back early from her trip.

4 Complete the text with words in the box. Use simple present or *will*.

arrive	call	do	get	graduate
leave	spend	start	take	

My best friend Sam and I ^{1}_____ from college in May. After we ^{2}_____ some time at home, we ^{3}_____ a really long trip to Europe. Before we ^{4}_____, we ^{5}_____ travel apps for our phones and we ^{6}_____ a lot of research. We ^{7}_____ in London. As soon as we ^{8}_____, we ^{9}_____ my cousin. He lives there and knows all the best places to see.

Present tenses for future plans and schedules ▶4.3

5 Read the sentences. Write *S* (schedule) or *P* (plan).

____ 1 The movie starts at 3:30.
____ 2 We're getting a coffee after class.
____ 3 Do you have class at 5:00 today?
____ 4 They're studying together later.
____ 5 He's bringing the reports with him.
____ 6 Where are they going to eat dinner?
____ 7 What time does the presentation start?
____ 8 I don't have an appointment at 2:00.

6 Choose the correct words to complete the sentences.

1 According to the website, the train *leaves* / *is going to leave* at noon.
2 Cindy and I *meet* / *are meeting* tomorrow.
3 The clients *come* / *are coming* at 3:00 p.m.
4 Matt *is calling* / *is going to call* sometime.
5 Greta *does* / *is going to do* yoga at 6:00 p.m. every day.
6 *Are you going to run* / *Do you run* with us tomorrow?

VOCABULARY DEVELOPMENT: Phrasal verbs: Separable and inseparable ▶4.1

1 Complete the sentences using words from the box.

across	away	into	off	out	up

1 You need to watch _____ for cars when you're running on this road.

2 I can't put _____ my travel plans any longer.

3 Did you throw _____ the gym schedule?

4 Let's look _____ a dance class.

5 Have you come _____ any good articles on exercise?

6 We stayed home last night. We ended _____ watching TV.

2 Rewrite the sentences to separate the phrasal verbs.

1 Can you **pick up** a schedule for me?

_____

2 He **put off** the test for another week.

_____

3 By mistake, I **threw away** the directions.

_____

4 She **brought up** possible exercise options.

_____

5 Who **put up** the sign for the parkour demonstration?

_____

6 Let's **try out** the new gym.

_____

3 Read the sentences. Do they use a phrasal verb or a verb + a prepositional phrase? Write *PV* (phrasal verb) or *VPP* (verb + prepositional phrase) on the lines.

____ 1 He came across the street to say hello.

____ 2 He came across a photo of his mother.

____ 3 They watched the game out on the grass.

____ 4 They watched out for trains as they drove across the tracks.

____ 5 We looked into a membership, but it was too expensive.

____ 6 We looked into the hole but couldn't see anything.

Traveling ▶4.2

4 Match the words with their definitions.

____ 1 baggage   ____ 5 reservation

____ 2 bargain   ____ 6 security

____ 3 economy   ____ 7 sights

____ 4 forecast

a something cheaper than usual

b procedures followed to keep people safe

c prediction about the weather

d a cheaper seat on a flight

e suitcases and bags for traveling

f places of interest to tourists and visitors

g an arrangement that holds something for you, for example, a seat

5 Choose the correct words to complete the sentences.

1 We made our *sights / reservations* for the train online.

2 Flights to Sydney are a real *economy / bargain* right now.

3 The Colosseum is one of the most popular *sights / baggage* in Rome.

4 I usually fly *security / economy*, but this time, I was in business class.

5 She never checks the *forecast / reservations* before she travels, so she often has the wrong clothes.

6 Have you ever lost your *baggage / bargains*? The airlines will sometimes pay for your clothes.

7 It takes a long time to go through *forecast / security* at the airport.

6 Complete the text with the correct words from Exercise 4.

My brother and I are taking a vacation together next month. He likes to save money, so he's looking for a ¹_____ online. He always flies ²_____. Sometimes the flight is cheaper if you don't have a ³_____ for a specific seat. That makes me nervous. I want to know exactly where I'll be sitting and when I'll be flying. I don't want to miss seeing any of the ⁴_____. One problem with trying to save money is that you usually can't carry lots of ⁵_____ with you. At least that makes it easy to go through ⁶_____!

REAL-WORLD READING

1 Read the blog post. Complete the sentence.

The blog post describes _____ tourism.

 ## Are you a responsible tourist?

Although tourism is generally good for a country's economy, providing jobs and money, it can also cause problems.

Did you know?

- International tourists may number 1.8 billion by 2030.
- Ten thousand people arrive on vacations daily in Mexico where trash is thrown away, not recycled.
- A single hotel in the U.S. desert will use 12 million liters of water next year.
- By 2050, as many as 30% of today's plants and animals could disappear because of human activity.

What's responsible tourism?

Sustainable tourism reduces tourism's impact on the environment and local communities. Sustainability

issues range from the management of natural resources (waste, water, energy, etc.), to the enjoyment of tourists, preservation of culture, and addressing climate change.

We should only use resources such as clean water and energy if they can be replaced at the same rate (or faster). We also shouldn't pollute faster than our ability to clean up after ourselves.

For my next vacation, I'm looking into hotels that don't wash their towels every day, and ones that use solar or wind power. I'm taking a reusable water bottle, so I won't have to throw away a lot of ugly plastic. When I travel, I'll take public transportation or rent a bike instead of renting a car. I think these small steps will be good for everyone!

—Adapted from *A Dictionary of Travel and Tourism* by Allan Beaver

2 Check four sentences that best state the four main ideas of the blog post.

☐ Tourism can cause problems.
☐ Tourism uses resources.
☐ Ten thousand people go on vacation in Mexico every year.
☐ Sustainable tourism reduces the negative impact on the environment and community.
☐ The enjoyment of tourists is also important.
☐ Some kinds of energy are more sustainable than others.
☐ The writer plans to be more environmentally friendly on his next vacation.
☐ The writer is going to take a reusable water bottle.

3 Complete the chart with the examples of tourism practices in the box.

rent a bike	use public transportation	use wind power	recycle
rent a car	use water without replacing it	wash towels every day	pollute
use solar power	throw plastic away		

Sustainable tourism practice	Not sustainable tourism practice

4 Complete the sentences with information from the blog post.

1 There may be _____ international tourists by 2030.

2 A hotel in the U.S. desert will use 12 million liters _____ next year.

3 As many as _____ percent of plants and animals may disappear by 2050.

4 _____ are natural resources.

5 We should _____ resources as fast as we use them.

6 _____ are sustainable power sources.

7 Using a reusable bottle prevents the waste of a lot of _____.

8 Public transportation is more sustainable than _____.

READING SKILL: Separating fact and opinion ▶4.2

5 Read the sentences from the blog post. Do they show fact or opinion?
Write *F* (fact) or *O* (opinion).

____ 1 Although tourism is generally good for a country's economy, providing jobs and money, it can also cause problems.

____ 2 International tourists may number 1.8 billion by 2030.

____ 3 Ten thousand people arrive on vacations daily in Mexico, where trash is thrown away, not recycled.

____ 4 A single hotel in the U.S. desert will use 12 million liters of water next year.

____ 5 By 2050, as many as 30% of today's plants and animals could disappear because of human activity.

____ 6 Sustainable tourism reduces tourism's impact on the environment and local communities.

____ 7 We should only use resources such as clean water and energy if they can be replaced at the same rate.

____ 8 I'm taking a reusable water bottle, so I won't have to throw away a lot of ugly plastic.

____ 9 I think these small steps will be good for everyone!

6 Look at your answers in Exercise 5. Complete the sentences with *fact/facts* or *opinion/opinions*.

1 _____ often use numbers.

2 You can prove _____.

3 When you use adjectives like *terrible* or *good*, you are probably expressing a(n) _____.

4 Expressions like *I think* or *in my view* usually introduce _____.

5 Information like dates and amounts are usually _____.

6 You can't prove _____ because other people may think differently.

7 When people use *should*, they are usually expressing a(n) _____.

REAL-WORLD ENGLISH: Being a customer ▶4.4

1 Complete the conversation from the video with the words in the box.

| Anything else | get you | How's it | I'm good | medium | That's all |

Sarah: Hey. ¹_____ going?

Andy: Hey, Sarah. ²_____, thanks.

Sarah: Great. What can I ³_____?

Andy: Oh, I'll have a green tea and a ⁴_____ coffee, please.

Saray: Green tea and a coffee. ⁵_____?

Andy: No. ⁶_____. Thank you.

2 Match the expressions used together in the video.

1 Just a minute! _____   a I'm not in a hurry.

2 Take this one. _____   b I'll be right with you.

3 Can I pay you later? _____   c Why not?

4 Sure. _____   d Gotta go!

3 Put the following conversation in order.

_____ Could I have a small coffee, please? And a banana muffin?

_____ No, thanks. That's all.

_____ Good morning. Welcome to Coffee First. How are you today?

_____ Great. How can I help you?

_____ Of course. A small coffee and a banana muffin. Anything else?

_____ Good, thank you. And you?

4 Match the expressions with their purposes.

_____ 1 No, thank you. That'll be it.   a greeting

_____ 2 Hello. How are you this morning?   b thanks / finish

_____ 3 A bran muffin and a small coffee? Anything else?   c confirmation of order

_____ 4 Good. How can I help you today?   d request for service

_____ 5 I'd like a bran muffin and a small coffee, please.   e offer of service

_____ 6 Great, thanks. And you?   f response to greeting

5 Are the expressions formal? Choose *Yes* or *No*.

	Yes	No
1 How are you today?	☐	☐
2 A large coffee and a bagel.	☐	☐
3 Great, thanks. I'm in a hurry.	☐	☐
4 Large green tea and banana muffin. Anything else?	☐	☐
5 What's up?	☐	☐
6 I'll have a large green tea, please.	☐	☐
7 Thank you so much.	☐	☐
8 So I have a large green tea and a banana muffin. Would you like anything else?	☐	☐

@ **GO ONLINE to listen to the podcast from the Unit Review.**

1 🔊 Listen to the Unit Review Podcast. What topic are they discussing?

2 🔊 Listen to the podcast again. Choose *True, False* or *Not Given*.

		True	False	Not Given
1	Michael and Nadia are students.	☐	☐	☐
2	Nadia thinks that good health is physical and mental.	☐	☐	☐
3	Michael says exercise helps your thinking skills.	☐	☐	☐
4	Exercise increases stress.	☐	☐	☐
5	When we move, our brains become active, too.	☐	☐	☐
6	Michael plans to go skiing this weekend.	☐	☐	☐

3 🔊 Listen to the podcast again. Complete the sentences with the words in the box.

bargain	body	exercise	ideas	mood	outdoors	Nadia

1 _____ wants to strengthen the connection between mind and _____.

2 When Nadia exercises, her _____ improves.

3 Walking _____ makes Michael more productive, and he gets good _____.

4 Nadia wants to _____ four or five times a week.

5 Outdoor exercise is a _____ because you can walk or bike for free.

LISTENING SKILL: Recognizing reductions with *to* ▶4.1

4 🔊 Listen to the sentences from the podcast. Do you hear the reduced form or the full form of the underlined phrases?

		Reduced	Full
1	Nadia, what are you going to do to be healthier?	☐	☐
2	I'm going to work on strengthening the connection between mind and body.	☐	☐
3	For example, I need to do some writing today.	☐	☐
4	This year, I want to exercise four or five times a week.	☐	☐
5	And I'm going to try out some new outdoor activities.	☐	☐
6	True, you might have to check the forecast more often.	☐	☐
7	But at least you won't have to make a reservation.	☐	☐
8	I'm not going to put off getting fit any longer.	☐	☐

DISCUSSION BOARD PREPARATION

5 Look at the Unit 4 Review Discussion Point. Read the questions in the prompt. Then read the reply. What motivates the writer to move?

_____

6 How do the writer's mind and body affect each other? What is he going to do to improve his mind-body connection?

_____

Unit 4 Review Discussion Point

1   Read the quote. What motivates you to be active? For example, to travel, to exercise, or to do sports?
"Whenever the urge to exercise comes upon me, I lie down for a while and it passes."
—Robert Maynard Hutchins, selected from *The Oxford Dictionary of American Quotations*, 2nd ed., edited by Hugh Rawson and Margaret Miner
2   In what ways do your mind and body affect each other?
3   Do you do anything to help your mind and body connect? If so, what? What will you do in the future to improve the connection between your mind and body?

Latest: **Ben**
one hour ago
I want to live a healthy and full life. That motivates me to travel and to exercise. My mind and body influence each other to be active. When I feel strong physically, I also feel confident and creative. When I am sick or out of shape, I put off exercising. I also don't feel as happy. When I'm sad or afraid, I often feel tired and end up watching TV instead of going out and doing things. I have to watch out when I start to feel this way, or I will get depressed. When I notice that I feel sad, I try to exercise because I know it's going to help me feel better.
   I do several things to help my mind and body connect. For example, this week I'll go to yoga a few times. I'll also try to meditate and be mindful of what is going on around me. I'm going to focus on the present, so I feel less stress. I'm also going to get outside. Walking in the park makes me feel positive and relaxed. My body and my mind need to work together for good health. Movement really helps both mind and body.

7   Overall, did the writer answer all the questions? If yes, explain. If no, what can the writer change? Then use the rubric to give a score for the reply. Give points: 0 (not successful)– 10 (successful).

_____

_____

Writing a Discussion Board Post	Points
The post answers the questions clearly and completely.	
The post has a general opening sentence and a general closing sentence.	
The post uses grammar and vocabulary from the unit.	
The post shows careful thinking about the topic.	
Sentences are complete and have correct punctuation.	
The post is long enough (180–220 words).	
Total	

WRITE YOUR POST

8   Read the quote. What motivates you to be active? For example, to travel, to exercise, or to do sports? In what ways do your mind and body affect each other? Do you do anything to help your mind and body connect? If so, what? What will you do in the future to improve the connection between your mind and body? Write a draft of your post for the Unit 4 Review Discussion Board.

 "Whenever the urge to exercise comes upon me, I lie down for a while and it passes."
—Robert Maynard Hutchins, selected from *The Oxford Dictionary of American Quotations*, 2nd ed., edited by Hugh Rawson and Margaret Miner

9   Use the rubric from Exercise 7 to score your post. Then improve your post.

 Go ONLINE to add your comments to the discussion board.

5 Home

Making comparisons ▶5.1

1 Choose the correct words to complete the sentences.

1 I think yellow is *less / the least* attractive than blue.
2 A messy room is not as restful *than / as* a clean one.
3 A new paint job is one of *easier / the easiest* ways to change the look of your home.
4 Adam's home is *more / most* spacious than mine.
5 The *more / most* important factor to me in an office is the number of windows.
6 It doesn't matter which color you use. The light blue is *just / not* as relaxing as the blue-green.

2 Complete the sentences with the correct forms of the adjectives in parentheses.

1 The living room is _____ (large) room in my house.
2 That blue isn't _____ (relaxing) as the green.
3 I like to use _____ (bright) lights during the winter because it's often cloudy.
4 One of _____ (good) ways to reduce stress is cleaning your house.
5 Tina is _____ (productive) when she works at the library than when she studies at home.
6 Unlike Tina, Jae is just _____ (hard-working) when studying at home.

Using two or more adjectives ▶5.2

3 Match the adjectives with the types.

1	old	____	a opinion
2	glass	____	b size
3	beautiful	____	c age
4	cutting	____	d shape
5	small	____	e color
6	round	____	f origin
7	Swedish	____	g material
8	red	____	h purpose

4 Write the adjectives in the correct order.

1 apartment / attractive / modern / building

_____

2 pot / small / coffee / metal

_____

3 Chinese / rug / old / red-and-blue / expensive

_____

4 green / comfortable / chair / oversized / reading

_____

5 Ethiopian / furniture / young / designer / talented

_____

6 cotton / dirty / white / shirt / Egyptian

_____

-ed and -ing adjectives ▶5.3

5 Choose the correct words to complete the sentences.

1 Are you *interested / interesting* in going to the museum?
2 I want to travel for a few weeks. It will be *bored / boring* to stay here all summer.
3 The news about the changes in the company is *worried / worrying*.
4 Do you have any *amused / amusing* stories about your trip?
5 Abad was very *pleased / pleasing* with his grade.
6 How *tired / tiring* is your dance class?

6 Complete the text with the *-ed* or *-ing* adjective forms of the words in the box.

disappoint	excite	interest	relax	stress	tire

My friend Ben and I just returned from a trip to Kyoto. We were so ¹_____ to see this beautiful city, and we weren't ²_____. I'm ³_____ in architecture, so I wanted to see the traditional buildings. There are also many beautiful gardens, and the use of fountains and other water features has a ⁴_____ effect—you can't feel ⁵_____ with the calming sound of water. We were very ⁶_____ at the end of the day because we walked so much. Fortunately, our hotel was nearby.

VOCABULARY

Expressions with *make* ▶5.1

1 Complete the sentences with *make* and the phrases in the box.

changes	a difference	an effort	sense	space

1 When I make _____ to organize my desk,
  I always feel better.

2 Elissa is getting rid of some old clothes to make
  _____ for new ones.

3 Relaxing colors like blue can really make _____
  in your level of stress.

4 It doesn't make _____ to spend a lot of money
  on the house because we are going to move in a year.

5 My company is making _____ to the office.
  They're removing some walls and adding windows.

2 Complete the conversations. Use an expression with *make*.

1 A: Wow! This kitchen is really dirty.
  B: Yeah, when we bake cookies, we usually
     _____.

2 A: What's the best way to save energy?
  B: Adding solar panels can really _____.

3 A: What does your roommate do that bothers you?
  B: He never _____, so his blankets look messy.

4 A: Why does your home always looks so beautiful?
  B: Well, I really _____. Thank you for noticing!

5 A: Why don't you paint your room?
  B: I don't like to _____, even little ones like
     painting the walls.

VOCABULARY DEVELOPMENT: Nouns and prepositions ▶5.2

3 Write the prepositions (*in, for, to, of*) used with the nouns.

1 access ____   5 change ____

2 description ____   6 reference ____

3 demand ____   7 member ____

4 advertisement ____   8 interest ____

4 Complete the sentences with a noun and preposition combination from Exercise 3.

1 Do you have any _____ living in a small town?

2 Look at this _____ a new apartment complex!
  They're showing model apartments today.

3 In the new apartment, we'll have _____ a gym
  24 hours a day.

4 Did they give you a _____ the neighborhood?
  What's it like?

5 There's a big _____ two-bedroom apartments.
  They are the most popular.

6 When you call about the house, tell them it's in
  _____ the ad you saw online.

7 You have to be a _____ the club to swim there.

8 There's going to be a _____ the fees for the
  neighborhood association. They're increasing 100%.

Phrasal verbs ▶5.3

5 Read the pairs of expressions. Are their meanings similar or different? Write *S* (similar) or *D* (different).

1 hurry up   slow down   ____

2 get rid of   throw away   ____

3 figure out   understand   ____

4 catch up   chat   ____

5 settle down   travel   ____

6 check on   ignore   ____

6 Choose the correct phrasal verbs to complete the text.

I never really felt at home until we became parents.
I used to travel a lot for work and fun, but I had to [1]*settle down / catch up* when our first baby was born. At first, I was very worried and [2]*caught up / checked on* the baby all the time. But soon we [3]*figured out / got rid of* how to manage our new routines. Sometimes in the morning we have to [4]*hurry up / settle down*, so we are not late. Although we are very busy, we always set aside time at the end of the day to [5]*catch up / check on*. Now that our children are a little older, we can [6]*hurry up / get rid of* the baby things.

1 Read the article. Complete the sentence.

Green architecture is _____.

Building Green

One of the more influential trends in architecture today is known as sustainable, or "green" architecture. What is green architecture, exactly? Its purpose is to establish a more cooperative, less environmentally damaging relationship between buildings and the environment. Architects can do this by making changes in fossil fuel use. If we get rid of or reduce our use of fossil fuels in the construction and operation of buildings, we can really make a difference. This means adopting a "whole life" strategy for the building, starting with construction, continuing through its lifetime, and ending with the destruction of the building.

The law of the "Three Rs" is most important: reduce, reuse, recycle. First, we waste as little as possible, so we reduce the materials we use. Second, because we design the building to work for as long as possible and use sustainable sources of energy, we are able to reuse it. Last, since the building is easy to take apart, we can recycle materials elsewhere.

In the operation of a building, we use two strategies: first, we reduce the demand for energy through the building design (e.g., thicker walls, a different position to protect it from the wind or sun); and second, supplying the remaining demand, as far as possible, with renewable energies (sun, wind, water, geothermal).

—Adapted from *The Oxford Companion to Architecture* edited by Patrick Goode

2 Read the article again. Use the information from the article to match the beginnings and endings of the sentences.

1	The purpose of green architecture is	___	a waste as little as possible.
2	A "whole life" strategy includes	___	b means that people can reuse the buildings.
3	One way to reduce materials is to	___	c taken apart and used elsewhere.
4	Creating buildings to last a long time	___	d to be better for the environment.
5	You can recycle if buildings can be	___	e its construction, lifetime, and destruction.
6	You can reduce energy demand with	___	f water and geothermal.
7	Examples of renewable energy are	___	g thicker walls.

3 Read the article again. Are the statements True, False, or Not Given?

		True	False	Not Given
1	Green architecture is an influential trend.	☐	☐	☐
2	Europe has more green buildings that anywhere else.	☐	☐	☐
3	Green buildings damage the environment less.	☐	☐	☐
4	Green buildings are built to last forever.	☐	☐	☐
5	Thinner walls reduce a building's energy use.	☐	☐	☐
6	Fossil fuels are a renewable source of energy.	☐	☐	☐
7	Using solar energy in the building helps the environment.	☐	☐	☐
8	Wind power is the most common energy used for homes.	☐	☐	☐

REAL-WORLD READING

READING SKILL: Recognizing cause and effect ▶5.1

4 Read the article again. Choose the correct options to complete the sentences about causes and effects.

1 Green architecture is an influential trend _____.

   a as it creates a cooperative relationship between buildings and the environment

   b so it creates a cooperative relationship between buildings and the environment

2 Architects make changes in fossil fuel use _____.

   a so buildings will be less environmentally damaging

   b because buildings are less environmentally damaging

3 Architects reduce the amount of materials they use _____.

   a so they waste as little as possible

   b because they waste as little as possible

4 People are able to reuse a building _____.

   a so it will last for a long time

   b as it is designed to last for a long time

5 Since green architects make buildings easy to take apart _____.

   a they can be recycled elsewhere

   b so they can be recycled elsewhere

6 Architects put a building in a different position _____.

   a so they can protect it from the sun or wind

   b because they reduce the building's energy use

7 Architects use renewable energy _____.

   a so building operation will be as green as possible

   b as building operation is as green as possible

5 Read the article again. Match the causes with the effects. They may not be clearly stated in the article.

1 Green architecture leads to ____   a the use of fewer materials.

2 Thicker walls result in ____   b reduced energy use.

3 A different building location provides ____   c can be moved and used elsewhere.

4 Reduced use of fossil fuels leads to ____   d a better environment.

5 A design that is easy to take apart ____   e protection from sun or wind.

6 Creating less waste results in ____   f a more cooperative relationship between buildings and the environment

REAL-WORLD ENGLISH: Making an invitation; accepting and rejecting invitations ▶5.4

1 Put the conversation from the video in order.

_____ Wow, that's nice of you.

_____ Yeah! Yeah, I'd love to.

_____ Yeah. Phil is having a surprise birthday party for Sam tonight.

_____ The latest soccer video game. Sam doesn't have it. Huh, I don't have it either!

_____ Hey! Is that a present?

_____ Cool. What is it?

_____ Thanks. Anyway, I can bring a guest. Would you like to come?

2 Match the lines in the conversation from the video with the functions in the box. Some lines have more than one function.

make an excuse	confirm	ask about availability	suggest an alternative
introduce the event	give more detail	invite	ask for details
give best wishes	say thank you	accept refusal	

1 So are you two doing anything tonight? _____

2 There's a good movie playing at 7:00. Do you two want to go? _____

3 Oh, thanks, but we're going to a surprise birthday party for Sam. _____

4 Oh, OK. Maybe another time. _____

5 Well, how about tomorrow night? _____

6 Sure. What time are you thinking? _____

7 Seven? _____

8 OK. Sounds great. Enjoy the snacks. See you! _____

3 Read the following conversation, and answer the questions.

Hugo: Hey, Roger. I'm going to get a coffee. Want to join me?

Roger: Hello, Hugo. Oh, I'm sorry. That is so very kind of you, but I have a class soon.

Hugo: That's OK. We can do it another time.

Roger: Again, I'm so sorry I can't make it today. Would you be free tomorrow?

Hugo: Sure. Same time?

Roger: Could we go just a little later? Perhaps 10:30?

Hugo: Works for me. See you at 10:30 then.

Roger: Thanks, that's great. I'm looking forward to catching up.

1 Who makes the invitation? _____

2 What is the excuse? _____

3 Who suggests an alternative? _____

4 What alternative do they agree on? _____

5 Who thanks the other speaker? _____

6 Who makes a positive comment? What is it? _____

7 Which speaker is more formal? Why do you think so? _____

UNIT REVIEW: Podcast

> Go online to listen to the podcast from the Unit Review.

1 Listen to the Unit Review Podcast. Are the statements True, False, or Not Given?

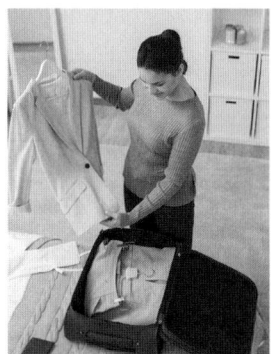

		True	False	Not Given
1	Sara Platt is a friend of the podcast host.	☐	☐	☐
2	To feel at home, Sara packs her favorite things.	☐	☐	☐
3	Dr. Ansuwar uses the Internet to meet people on trips.	☐	☐	☐
4	Dr. Ansuwar recommends eating and sleeping well.	☐	☐	☐

2 Listen to the podcast again. Choose the correct phrases to complete the sentences.

1 Dr. Ansuwar is _____.

  a the podcast host   b a co-host   c a psychologist

2 Sara apologizes for _____.

  a missing a podcast   b being late   c forgetting to call in

3 Sara often brings _____ with her on trips.

  a a camera   b comfortable pajamas   c a pillow

4 Dr. Ansuwar says you can feel more connected when traveling if you _____.

  a know people   b bring a laptop   c use your phone

LISTENING SKILL: Distinguishing levels of formality ▶5.3

3 Listen to the lines from the podcast. Choose the characteristics for the lines from the podcast. Which sentences are informal? Why?

	Sentences		Vocabulary	
	Short	Long	Idiomatic	Standard
1 Me too. Sorry I missed the last one. Everything in China is earlier.				
2 I make an effort to bring my favorite stuff with me.				
3 I'm more relaxed that way.				
4 On social media, you can find descriptions of places to stay that will allow you to feel more comfortable.				
5 Having acquaintances in a new place can help you feel less stressed and more connected.				

DISCUSSION BOARD PREPARATION

4 Look at the Unit 5 Review Discussion Point. Read the questions in the prompt. Then read the reply. What examples does the writer give to show the meaning of *home*?

_____

5 What places make the writer feel at home? What other things make him feel at home?

_____

Unit 5 Review Discussion Point

1 Read the quote. Is home a place or a feeling?
"Some books are so familiar that reading them is like being home again."
—Louisa May Alcott, selected from *The Oxford Dictionary of American Quotations*, 2nd ed.,
edited by Hugh Rawson and Margaret Miner
2 When do you feel most at home? Why?

Latest: Carlo Petrelli
two days ago
I think home can be both a place and a feeling. When I am in a familiar, well-loved place, I feel comfortable and at home. For example, when I return to my parents' cozy little house, I feel like I'm coming home. I know where everything is, and I have many happy memories there. I'm surrounded by familiar faces and objects. However, I also feel at home when I am with close friends and family, even if I'm in a strange place. I think the feeling is more important than the place.

I feel most at home when I'm not anxious or stressed. I have to be comfortable in order to feel at home. When I have to hurry up and get things done, I can't rest. But when I can settle down and relax in a beautiful, calm setting surrounded by favorite things and people, I can feel at home even if I am traveling. Sometimes I feel at home when I reread a good book, watch an old movie, or eat a traditional Italian meal, complete with pasta and tiramisu.

6 Overall, did the writer answer all the questions? If yes, explain. If no, what can the writer change? Then use the rubric to give a score for the reply. Give points: 0 (not successful)– 10 (successful).

Writing a Discussion Board Post	Points
The post answers the questions clearly and completely.	
The post has a general opening sentence and a general closing sentence.	
The post uses grammar and vocabulary from the unit.	
The post shows careful thinking about the topic.	
Sentences are complete and have correct punctuation.	
The post is long enough (180–220 words).	
Total	

WRITE YOUR POST

7 Read the quote. Is home a place or a feeling? When do you feel most at home? Why? Write a draft of your post for the Unit 5 Review Discussion Board.

"Some books are so familiar that reading them is like being home again."
—Louisa May Alcott, selected from
The Oxford Dictionary of American Quotations, 2nd ed., edited by
Hugh Rawson and Margaret Miner

8 Use the rubric from Exercise 6 to score your post. Then improve your post.

 Go ONLINE to add your comments to the discussion board.

6 Images

Quantifiers: *Both, several, most,* and *all* ▶6.1

1 Choose the correct words to complete the sentences.

1 There have been *several / both* moon landings guided by astronauts.

2 On *all of / all* them, a third astronaut stayed on board the whole time.

3 *Most / Both* of the other astronauts walked on the moon's surface.

4 Although there are many photos of the earth, *most / both* of them were taken by satellites.

5 *Most / Most of* the walks on the moon lasted more than five hours.

2 Complete the sentences with the words in the box.

all	all of	both	most of	several

1 _____ nations have sent manned spaceships into space—the U.S., Russia, and China.

2 At least ten countries have the ability to launch ships into space. _____ ten have launched satellites.

3 _____ the satellites in space now belong to the U.S., China, and Russia. Other nations own fewer than half.

4 The U.S. has more satellites than _____ China and Russia.

5 _____ us benefit from satellite images. They provide information for GPS and other technologies.

Quantifiers: *Too much / too many, a little / a few, a lot, enough* ▶6.2

3 Match the quantifiers with their uses.

____ 1 enough   ____ 4 too much

____ 2 a few   ____ 5 too many

____ 3 a little   ____ 6 a lot of

a small amount of a countable noun

b small amount of an uncountable noun

c large amount of countable and uncountable nouns

d more of a countable noun than we need

e more of an uncountable noun than we need

f all that is necessary

4 Complete the sentences with the words in the box.

a few	a lot of	too many
too much	enough	a little

1 There are _____ people in this photo. You can't see all their faces.

2 I can't save these photos. I don't have _____ memory on my phone.

3 _____ people post photos on the Internet, but I don't like to.

4 She only looks good in _____ of the photos. In most of them, her eyes are closed.

5 This photo looks pale. There's _____ light.

6 Can you give me _____ advice on taking photos? Just a tip or two?

Verbs with two objects ▶6.3

5 Rewrite the sentences. Don't use *to* or *for*.

1 He printed a ticket for the passenger.

_____

2 Wei gave a copy of the guidebook to his friend.

_____

3 Gina sent photos of her trip to her family.

_____

4 Can you save a place for me on the tour?

_____

5 The architect built a model of the building for us.

_____

6 Write the words in the correct order to make sentences.

1 I / my co-worker / the details / emailed / to

_____

2 made / us / the hotel clerk / reservations

_____

3 the clients / her design / to / showed / the architect

_____

4 Mark's boss / a souvenir / from / Paris / brought / him

_____

5 book / flights / you / can / us / for

_____?

VOCABULARY DEVELOPMENT:
Agent nouns ▶6.1

1 Write the agent nouns for the words.
Use *-er*, *-or*, *-ist*, or *-ian*.

1 art   _____

2 edit   _____

3 explore   _____

4 govern   _____

5 music   _____

6 photograph   _____

7 politics   _____

8 science   _____

9 paint   _____

10 history   _____

2 Complete the sentences with the words from Exercise 1.

1 A(n) _____ studies past events.

2 A(n) _____ usually plays an instrument, for example, a piano or a guitar.

3 A _____ is a kind of _____—one who uses paint on some kind of surface.

4 Biologists are a kind of _____. They study biology.

5 Some _____ work in government in official positions like president or _____. Others work behind the scenes in supporting roles.

6 A(n) _____ goes to new places, often ones that very few people have visited.

7 Newspapers employ a lot of people. They need _____ to take pictures and _____ to make sure the articles are well-written.

3 Do you recognize these people? Match the people with the agent nouns.

1 Vincent Van Gogh   ____   a singer

2 Toni Morrison   ____   b scientist

3 Marie Curie   ____   c novelist

4 Ansel Adams   ____   d photographer

5 Andrea Bocelli   ____   e painter

Photos ▶6.2

4 Match the descriptions with the correct expressions in the box.

landscape photo	photo frame	in focus
use a flash	out of focus	use a selfie stick
a view	a portrait	

1 This is a way to display your pictures. You can put it on your wall or set it on a desk or table. _____

2 Sometimes there isn't enough light for a good photo. Then you need to do this. _____

3 People often take these when they travel. They show what the countryside looks like. _____

4 This describes a photo that is very clear. _____

5 This describes a photo in which some things are fuzzy or unclear. _____

6 Sometimes people take photos of themselves with a phone. They often need to do this to get the phone far enough away. _____

7 This is a photo of a person or people. _____

8 This is something, often attractive, that you can see from a particular place. _____

5 Look at the photo. Are the sentences correct? Check *True* or *False*.

		True	False
1	This photo is **in focus**.	☐	☐
2	The cyclist is **out of focus**.	☐	☐
3	There is a **view**.	☐	☐
4	The photographer used a **selfie stick**.	☐	☐
5	The photographer had to use a **flash**.	☐	☐

READING SKILL: Recognizing prefixes ▶6.2

1 Read the article. Complete the sentence.

Something beautiful appeals to _____ and makes you _____.

 ## What makes something beautiful?

People are attracted to beauty, whether it is in people, nature, or a landscape painting. But how do we know something is beautiful?

The branch of philosophy dealing with beauty, especially in art, is called *aesthetics*. Many philosophers associate aesthetic perception with the senses. However, according to traditional theories, not all of the senses let us appreciate aesthetic objects. In general, philosophers think sight and hearing are the aesthetic senses, and smell, taste, and touch are non-aesthetic. There are two reasons for this. First, the pleasures of smell, taste, and touch focus on your own personal feelings and so don't provide enough distance to appreciate the object itself. Second, the objects attractive to the bodily senses are considered inappropriate for the fine arts. Food, perfume, etc. can be practical or decorative only, unlike photography, painting, music, and dance, which are fine arts that appeal to sight and hearing.

True aesthetic perception, however, also involves using your mind. Some thinkers say that aesthetic beauty requires a viewer to compare artwork like a portrait or a landscape with an original subject. Others disagree, saying appreciation of most natural objects, like a butterfly or a sunset, involves understanding, too. Nowadays, many are reconsidering the role of emotion in appreciating beauty. A talented musician or writer can make you both feel and think.

—Adapted from *Encyclopedia of Aesthetics*, 2nd ed., edited by Michael Kelly

2 Read the sentences from the article. What do the underlined prefixes mean? Choose the correct answers.

1 In general, philosophers think sight and hearing are the aesthetic senses, and smell, taste, and touch are non-aesthetic.
   a not, without   b in, within   c again

2 Second, the objects that appeal to the bodily senses are considered inappropriate for the fine arts.
   a into   b self   c not

3 Food, perfume, etc. can be practical or decorative only, unlike photography, painting, music, and dance, which are fine arts that appeal to sight and hearing.
   a in the middle   b not   c under

4 Others disagree, saying appreciation of natural objects, like a butterfly or a sunset, involves understanding, too.
   a apart, not   b within   c do again

5 Nowadays, many are reconsidering the role of emotion vs. thinking in appreciating beauty.
   a not, without   b out, from   c again, back

3 Complete the sentences with the correct words with prefixes from Exercise 4.

1 The museum only shows oil paintings, so photographs would be a(n) _____ exhibit.

2 Many people think food is too common to be an art, but I _____.

3 I used to think classical music was boring, but now I'm _____ that opinion.

4 I prefer to eat a good dinner than go to an art museum, so I guess that's a(n) _____ choice.

5 _____ my sister who plays the piano, I have no musical talent at all.

4 Read the words from the article with new prefixes added. Match the words with their meanings.

____ 1 mid-distance   a not usual, new

____ 2 non-traditional   b a person who writes with another person

____ 3 misunderstanding   c not attractive

____ 4 unappealing   d failure to understand correctly

____ 5 disassociate   e not close and not far away

____ 6 impractical   f separate or split

____ 7 co-writer   g a person who looks at something again

____ 8 reviewer   h not useful

READING: Practice

5 Read the article again. Then complete the sentences with information from the article.

1 The branch of philosophy that deals with beauty is called _____.

2 According to philosophers, aesthetic senses are _____.

3 The non-aesthetic senses are _____.

4 Non-aesthetic senses focus on _____.

5 _____ and _____ can be practical or decorative.

6 _____ include photography, painting, music, and dance.

7 To really appreciate beauty you also have to use _____.

8 Two examples of artists that makes you feel as well as think include _____ and _____.

6 According to the article, what makes something aesthetic? Write *A* (aesthetic) and *N* (non-aesthetic).

1 hearing, seeing   _____   5 music, painting   _____

2 provides distance   _____   6 uses the mind   _____

3 food, perfume   _____   7 practical, decorative   _____

4 fine arts   _____

REAL-WORLD ENGLISH: Giving and accepting compliments ▶6.4

1 Match the compliments from the video with their responses.

1 Excellent work, Max! What a great portrait! _____

2 I really like the attention to detail! _____

3 That color blue looks good on you. _____

4 Hey, thanks. Nice jacket. I wish I had one like this. _____

5 It looks better on you than it does on me! _____

a Thanks, Andy! Wow, me. In a suit!

b Thanks. Ugh, I just need a suit now.

c Thanks! My sister helped me pick it out.

d Thanks, Emma. Do you really think so?

e Really? Thanks. I appreciate it.

2 Answer the questions about the responses to compliments in Exercise 1.

1 Which responses thank the other speaker? _____

2 Which responses give more details? _____

3 Which responses question the compliment? _____

4 Which responses return the compliment? _____

3 Read the compliment and the description in parentheses. Then match the strategies with the responses from the box.

"Your report for the client was really good." (boss to employee)

Was it clear enough?	I worked hard on it.	You gave me great notes.	Thank you so much.

1 Say thank you. _____

2 Give details. _____

3 Ask questions. _____

4 Return the compliment. _____

4 Read the conversation and answer the questions.

Store clerk: Hello. How can I help you?

Customer: I'm having trouble with the camera on my phone.

Store clerk: OK let's take a look. What seems to be the problem?

Customer: Look at these photos. Do they look out of focus to you?

Store clerk: Hmm. Not all of them are terrible. This is a great photo!

Customer: Really? Thanks. I took that with a selfie stick.

Store clerk: Good job! And this photo with a view of the bridge is not too bad.

Customer: Thanks, but I thought that looked out of focus.

Store clerk: But the person in front is in focus, so it works. It's a good photo overall.

Customer: That's nice to hear. I appreciate it. Are you a photographer, too?

1 What kind of store do you think this is?

_____

2 Which speaker gives compliments? What are the compliments?

_____

3 Which strategies are used to accept the compliments?

_____

UNIT REVIEW: Podcast

 Go online to listen to the podcast from the Unit Review.

1 🔊 Listen to the Unit Review Podcast. Are the statements True, False, or Not Given?

		True	False	Not Given
1	Photos always show how the world really is.	☐	☐	☐
2	Photographers don't express their own ideas.	☐	☐	☐
3	Technology allows us to change a photo.	☐	☐	☐
4	Most changes are made after the photograph is taken.	☐	☐	☐
5	Phone apps let us add funny hats to people in photos.	☐	☐	☐
6	Photography is like other art forms.	☐	☐	☐
7	People take more photos with phones than other cameras.	☐	☐	☐

2 🔊 Listen to the podcast again. Complete the text with information from the podcast.

Just like other ^{1}_____, ^{2}_____ use their art to express their own ^{3}_____ about the world. Sometimes this means changing what is actually there or at least what the ^{4}_____ sees. For example, through technology, we now have the ^{5}_____ to retouch photos immediately. We can remove red eyes that the ^{6}_____ produces, or brighten the photo if there's not enough natural light, or take out a spot or mark on someone's face. With regular cameras, sometimes a few objects are ^{7}_____, but others are blurry or ^{8}_____. However, technology allows us to create clear images of everything, even after the photo has been taken.

LISTENING SKILL: Listening for specific information ▶6.1

3 🔊 Listen to the podcast again. Complete the sentences with specific information from the podcast.

1 The podcast is called _____.

2 A flash sometimes produces _____.

3 When there isn't enough _____, we can brighten a photo.

4 We can add _____ to photos, or remove them.

5 The speaker's _____ couldn't attend the family reunion last year.

6 She used _____ to add the missing family member to the photo.

DISCUSSION BOARD PREPARATION

4 Look at the Unit 6 Review Discussion Point. Read the questions in the prompt. Then read the reply. What is the writer's opinion about the quote?

_____

5 What kinds of changes does the writer think are OK? What kinds of changes cause problems?

_____

Unit 6 Review Discussion Point

1 Read the quote. Do you agree?
"Photography is truth."
—Jean-Luc Godard, selected from *Oxford Dictionary of Quotations*, 8th ed., edited by Elizabeth Knowles
2 Is it always necessary for photographs to tell the truth?
3 When do photographs lie?

Latest: Lucy Kim
one hour ago
I agree in part and disagree in part. I think photography is truth in one way because all art is trying to say something true about the world. However, I don't think a photograph is always showing something that is a fact. For example, when I use an app to add funny ears to a photo of my friend, that is not exactly the way my friend looks.

I don't think it's always necessary for photographs to tell the truth. A few types of changes are fine. It's okay to change a photo to improve the way it looks, or to make something funny or entertaining. No one thinks the funny ears I put on my friend are real. It's a more serious problem when you add people into a photo, or take them out. In my opinion, news photos should always be accurate because people expect them to show exactly what is happening.

Photographs lie sometimes. For example, a news photo that shows a famous person in a situation that never happened is a lie. It can cause problems for that person, and that's not fair. Fake photos of monsters or spaceships may also confuse or scare people.

6 Overall, did the writer answer all the questions? If yes, explain. If no, what can the writer change? Then use the rubric to give a score for the reply. Give points: 0 (not successful)–10 (successful).

Writing a Discussion Board Post	Points
The post answers the questions clearly and completely.	
The post has a general opening sentence and a general closing sentence.	
The post uses grammar and vocabulary from the unit.	
The post shows careful thinking about the topic.	
Sentences are complete and have correct punctuation.	
The post is long enough (180–220 words).	
Total	

WRITE YOUR POST

7 Read the quote. Do you agree? Is it always necessary for photographs to tell the truth? When do photographs lie? Write a draft of your post for the Unit 6 Review Discussion Board.

"Photography is truth"
—Jean Luc-Godard, selected from *Oxford Dictionary of Quotations*,
8th ed., edited by Elizabeth Knowles

8 Use the rubric from Exercise 6 to score your post. Then improve your post.

 Go ONLINE to add your comments to the discussion board.

7 Predictions

Must, have to, and can't: Deductions about the present ▶7.1

1 Choose the correct words to complete the conversations.

1 A: Hong has texted me a dozen times already.
   B: She *must / can't* miss you.

2 A: Maria packed too much for school, and now she says her room is too small.
   B: Then she *has to / can't* have enough room for all of her stuff.

3 A: The screen on my new phone is really big.
   B: That *must / mustn't* make it easy to see.

4 A: I don't know what all these emojis mean.
   B: Then some texts *have to / can't* be confusing.

5 A: This text *has to / can't* be from Yuri. He promised to text right away.
   B: Let me see. No—it *mustn't / can't* be Yuri. That's not his phone number.

2 Complete the sentences with *can't* or *must*.

1 The text says, "Your apartment is at 1:00 p.m."
   It _____ mean "appointment."

2 Rob hasn't responded. He _____ have a class now.

3 Susana _____ be in Paris. I saw her this morning.

4 Luis _____ be buying a new phone already!
   He just bought one.

5 I missed five calls. My ringer _____ be off.

Will and might: Predictions ▶7.2

3 Choose the prediction that is more certain.

1 ___ a Phones will probably be smaller in the future.
   ___ b Phones might be bigger in the future.

2 ___ a Buildings might be taller.
   ___ b Buildings will definitely be taller.

3 ___ a I think people will live in big cities.
   ___ b People might not live near the coast.

4 ___ a People might not drive cars anymore.
   ___ b I don't believe people will drive anymore.

5 ___ a Houses probably won't have yards.
   ___ b Houses definitely won't have yards.

4 Complete the text with *will, won't, might,* or *might not.*

I think machines [1]_____ soon perform most routine jobs. It's almost certain. This means that many people [2]_____ be working in places like factories. However, people [3]_____ still need to make money. Because machines and robots [4]_____ definitely take jobs away, some people [5]_____ be able to work at all.

Here's a possibility: governments [6]_____ start giving people a certain amount of money to live on each month even if they don't work. This [7]_____ seem like a crazy idea at first. Some people [8]_____ want to work at all, but governments are going to have to try different solutions.

Adverbs: A little, pretty, much, and really ▶7.3

5 Choose the correct words to complete the sentences.

1 I'm a *pretty / little* nervous about learning grammar.

2 For me, English is *much / really* harder to learn than other languages.

3 Some languages will be *pretty / much* more popular than others in 50 years.

4 Online learning isn't a *really / little* effective way to learn a language, in my opinion.

5 It's *pretty / much* easy to learn a language when you live in a country where it is spoken.

6 Write the words in the correct order to make sentences.

1 other languages / has / than / longer words / German / much / many

   _____

2 about / a / is / my grade / my teacher / worried / little

   _____

3 really / the / hard / understand / lecture / was / to

   _____

4 pretty / online / convenient / learning / is

   _____

5 than / more / a little / this book / interesting / is / the last one

   _____

VOCABULARY DEVELOPMENT: Collocations with *get* ▶7.1

1 Read the sentences. Write the correct meaning of *get*: *receive*, *become*, *catch*, or *arrive*.

1 Karl got a cab immediately. _____

2 Ahmed gets to work before I do. _____

3 Ono gets angry easily. _____

4 How do you get a promotion? _____

5 I just got a text from Ricardo. _____

6 We got sick over the school break. _____

7 Don't get upset about little things. _____

8 They got a flight to Lisbon. _____

2 Match the questions with the answers.

1 Why are you two so late? ____

2 How did you get home? ____

3 Why did you tell Carlos in Spanish? ____

4 How did you find out about the job? ____

5 You look happy. What happened? ____

6 Did the medicine help? ____

7 Can you call when you're on your way? ____

8 How did you break your arm? ____

a I got injured playing soccer.

b We got a train from Central Station.

c Yes, she got better very quickly.

d I got a job!

e We got lost.

f I got an email about it.

g I might not get a chance.

h He gets confused sometimes in English.

3 Complete the sentences with the correct form of a collocation with *get*.

1 I _____ in the rainstorm. I need to _____ into something dry.

2 How long does it take you to _____ for work in the morning?

3 We didn't _____ to the party. I'm disappointed they didn't ask us to go.

4 When do you _____? I can stop by your house at 7:00.

5 Amira and Edward plan to _____ on June 3. Their wedding will be beautiful.

Predictions ▶7.2

4 Complete the sentences with the phrases in the box.

accurate	for certain	confident
doubt	evidence	as far as

1 It was a(n) _____ prediction. Everything he said was true.

2 He always wants to see the _____ before he'll believe something.

3 The information is true _____ I know, but I might not be well informed.

4 We seriously _____ that is true, as our research shows a different result.

5 I'm really _____ that those facts are correct.

6 We don't know _____, but we are pretty sure.

5 Choose the correct words to complete the sentences.

1 Are you *accurate* / *confident* that all cars will be driverless soon?

2 If the research is *accurate* / *confident*, most cars will not need a human driver.

3 There is a lot of *doubt* / *evidence* that proves our climate is changing.

4 *For certain* / *As far as* we know, there is no life on Mars.

5 I seriously *doubt* / *as far as* machines will be able to do all jobs.

6 She knew *accurate* / *for certain* that the man took her bag.

READING SKILL: Recognizing words with more than one meaning ▶7.1

1 Skim the article. Complete the sentence.

Science fiction both _____ and _____ scientific developments.

Science Fiction and the Future

Given the human love of storytelling, the rise of modern science inevitably prompted stories involving science. Mary Shelley wrote *Frankenstein,* one of the first science fiction novels, in 1818. After World War II, major writers crafted both realistic accounts of near-future developments and visions of humanity's distant future. In the 1970s, the *Star Trek* television series and *Star Wars* films made science fiction much more popular.

Science fiction often has a really strong relationship with the scientific community. Scientists such as Stephen Hawking and Carl Sagan have been inspired by science fiction. Evidence suggests the terms *astronaut, genetic engineering,* and *robotics* originated in science fiction stories. Science fiction not only has the ability to make accurate predictions about future inventions; it may also encourage scientific thinking and influence policy decisions. In the 1950s, novels and films portrayed human space flight—within two decades, people walked on the moon. Those events can't be unrelated. Imagining spaceflight helped us get ready to make it a reality.

Science fiction has also helped prevent scientific developments. The frightening technology in George Orwell's *Nineteen Eighty-Four* (1947) sparked efforts to prevent that future from being for certain. And since science fiction films have given us images of "mad scientists" whose projects lead to disasters, researchers today must proceed carefully, anticipating public fears of new "Frankenstein monsters."

—Adapted from *The Oxford Companion to the History of Modern Science* by J. L. Heilbron

2 Read the sentences from the article. What is the best meaning for the underlined word? Choose the correct answers.

1 Given the human love of storytelling, the rise of modern science inevitably prompted stories involving science.
   a to cause, or bring about   b to encourage someone to talk

2 After World War II, major writers crafted both realistic accounts of near-future developments and visions of humanity's distant future.
   a the state of being able to see   b a mental image

3 After World War II, major writers crafted both realistic accounts of near-future developments and visions of humanity's distant future.
   a financial records   b descriptions

4 Evidence suggests the terms *astronaut, genetic engineering,* and *robotics* originated in science fiction stories.
   a certain periods   b words or phrases

5 The frightening technology in George Orwell's *Nineteen Eighty-Four* (1947) sparked efforts to prevent that future from being for certain.
   a encouraged   b set on fire

3 Complete the sentences with the correct forms of the words in Exercise 2.

1   I'm having problems with my _____. I can't always see clearly.

2   Do you know what the _____ *bioengineering* means?

3   The movie *Star Wars* _____ my interest in science fiction.

4   Our nine-month school _____ ends next month.

5   Do you believe Han's _____ of the accident?

6   I was so nervous during my speech. The instructor had to _____ me.

7   What's your _____ of the future? Does it include a lot of technology?

8   There are mistakes in the _____. I think a lot of money is missing.

9   The burner on the stove _____ as soon as you turn the gas on.

10 The deadline _____ me to start my essay.

READING: Practice

4 Read the article again. Decide whether each sentence describes a main idea or a detail of the article. Write *M* (main idea) or *D* (detail).

1   The rise of modern science led to science fiction.   ____

2   Mary Shelley wrote one of the first science fiction novels.   ____

3   In the 1970s, television and movies made science fiction more popular.   ____

4   Science fiction has a strong connection to the scientific community.   ____

5   Some words and phrases came from science fiction.   ____

6   Science fiction may encourage scientific thinking and influence policy.   ____

7   In the 1950s, novels and films portrayed space flight.   ____

8   Science fiction has also helped prevent scientific developments.   ____

5 Read the article again. Then complete the sentences with information from the article.

1   Mary Shelley wrote *Frankenstein* in _____.

2   The television show _____ and the _____ films made science fiction more popular.

3   The scientists _____ and _____ were inspired by science fiction.

4   Terms that come from science fiction include _____, _____, and _____.

5   Novels and movies in the 1950s showing _____ may have inspired people to walk on the moon.

6   George Orwell wrote _____, a novel with technology that frightened people.

7   Images of _____ caused researchers to proceed carefully.

1 Complete the conversation from the video with words in the box.

about that	do you think	I think	Really	should I take	You're right

Sam: So which workshop ¹_____ first? Writing for the Law or Reading

Strategies?

Andy: What ²_____, Jenna?

Jenna: Well, ³_____ reading strategies are very important. That workshop

helped me a lot.

Andy: ⁴_____. I'm thinking about taking that one first.

Sam: ⁵_____? I'm not sure ⁶_____. It sounds so boring.

2 Match the expressions with the functions.

_____ 1 I'm not sure about that.   a disagreeing more directly

_____ 2 Well, that's a good point, but ... .   b disagreeing less directly

_____ 3 Could you explain your thinking?   c accepting but disagreeing

_____ 4 Why do you say that?   d asking for an explanation more directly

_____ 5 I disagree completely.   e asking for an explanation less directly

3 Read the two conversations and answer the questions.

CONVERSATION 1

A: Some evidence suggests that the best way to learn a language is by reading a lot.

B: I'm not sure about that. Could you say more?

A: Well, reading will help you learn more vocabulary.

B: That's true, but don't you think you'll learn more quickly by talking to native speakers?

CONVERSATION 2

A: I think we should watch the movie instead of reading the whole book again.

B: Really? I disagree. They often change things in the movie.

A: That's a good point, but it would save time. And I have the movie on my phone.

B: Yeah, but don't you think we should review the book first? Then we'll watch the movie!

1 What is the relationship between the speakers?

_____

2 Which conversation is more formal?

_____

3 What expression is used to ask for explanations?

_____

4 What expressions are used to accept but disagree?

_____

5 What expressions are used to disagree?

_____

ENGLISH FOR REAL

LISTENING SKILL: Listening for main ideas ▶ 7.3

Go online and listen to the podcast from the Unit Review.

1 Listen to the Unit Review Podcast. Write *M* (main idea) or *D* (detail).

1 The podcast today is about delayed gratification. ____

2 The first studies on delayed gratification were in the 1960s. ____

3 Delayed gratification is influenced by both our genes and by the situation. ____

4 If you have doubt about the future reward, you'll take the immediate reward. ____

5 In the story, the ant works hard to save food for winter. ____

6 The grasshopper has a fun time. ____

7 People who delay gratification will be better prepared for their futures. ____

UNIT REVIEW: Podcast

2 Listen to the podcast again. Are the statements True, False, or Not Given?

		True	False	Not Given
1	In general, the podcast is about planning for the future.	☐	☐	☐
2	The last podcast was about retirement.	☐	☐	☐
3	The topic today is about career planning.	☐	☐	☐
4	Delayed gratification is waiting for a reward.	☐	☐	☐
5	The ability to wait is both genetic and environmental.	☐	☐	☐
6	The ability to wait is not related to future success.	☐	☐	☐
7	Women are better able to wait than men.	☐	☐	☐
8	The speaker uses a story to explain her ideas.	☐	☐	☐

3 Listen to the podcast again. Write the ideas in the correct place in the chart.

has fun now	doesn't save	goes on trips	works hard
saves for future	doesn't spend	gives up fun	has little in retirement

"Ant"	"Grasshopper"

DISCUSSION BOARD PREPARATION

4 Look at the Unit 7 Review Discussion Point. Read the questions in the prompt. Then read the reply. What is the writer's attitude toward planning for the future?

_____

5 Label the part of the reply that answers Question 1 from the prompt. Then label the parts that answer Question 2 and Question 3.

_____

Unit 7 Review Discussion Point

1   Read the quote. Do you like to plan for the future, or is it better to take life one day at a time?
"I never think of the future. It comes soon enough."
—Albert Einstein, selected from *Oxford Dictionary of Quotations*, 8th ed., edited by Elizabeth Knowles

2   How important is it to do without now in order to have more in the future?

3   What are you doing now that helps you prepare for the future?

Latest: Thien Nguyen
two hours ago
I like to prepare for the future as much as I can. I know some people take life one day at a time. I think they must be more relaxed, and they probably have much more fun. But I like to get ready for anything that might happen.

   Because I'm more like the ant, I think it's really important to do without some things now in order to have more in the future. Right now I'm young, and it's pretty easy to go back to school or change jobs if there's a problem. I could spend a lot of money on travel and entertainment and still pay my rent. I get a little nervous when I don't have a lot of money in my bank account.

   I'm doing a few things that help me prepare for the future. I save 5% of my paycheck in a retirement account. I also take classes because I think they will help me if I need to get a new job. I know sometimes bad things happen, so I have saved enough money to cover about six months of bills and other expenses.

6   Overall, did the writer answer all the questions? If yes, explain. If no, what can the writer change? Then use the rubric to give a score for the reply. Give points: 0 (not successful)–10 (successful).

Writing a Discussion Board Post	Points
The post answers the questions clearly and completely.	
The post has a general opening sentence and a general closing sentence.	
The post uses grammar and vocabulary from the unit.	
The post shows careful thinking about the topic.	
Sentences are complete and have correct punctuation.	
The post is long enough (180–220 words).	
Total	

WRITE YOUR POST

7   Read the quote. Do you like to plan for the future, or is it better to take life one day at a time? How important is it to do without now in order to have more in the future? What are you doing now that helps you prepare for the future? Write a draft of your post for the Unit 7 Review Discussion Board.

"I never think of the future. It comes soon enough."
—Albert Einstein, selected from *Oxford Dictionary of Quotations*, 8th ed., edited by Elizabeth Knowles

8   Use the rubric from Exercise 6 to score your post. Then improve your post.

   Go ONLINE to add your comments to the discussion board.

8 Consumption

Can, could, and may: Permission and requests ▶8.1

1 Read the sentences. Is the meaning formal or informal? Write *F* (formal) or *I* (informal).

___ 1 Could you help me find a size?

___ 2 May I get you a fitting room?

___ 3 Can I try this on?

___ 4 Can you show me your receipt?

___ 5 Customers may not try on more than three items at time.

___ 6 Could I return this if she doesn't like it?

2 Choose the correct words to complete the conversations.

1 A: *May / Could* you help me find a gift?
  B: Yes, I *can / may*.

2 A: *May not / Could* you make an exception?
  B: No, I *can't / could*.

3 A: *Can / Couldn't* I return this without a receipt?
  B: Yes, you *can / could*.

4 A: Shoppers *could not / may not* take drinks into the dressing rooms.
  B: *Could / May* you hold it for me at the register?

Be able to: Ability and possibility (present, past, and future) ▶8.2

3 Rewrite the sentences using the correct form of *be able to*.

1 Many people can't buy enough food to feed their families.

_____

2 In fact, nearly 800 million people worldwide couldn't get enough to eat in 2016.

_____

3 When people can't eat healthy food, they often get sick.

_____

4 Supermarkets and restaurants can help reduce hunger by giving food to charities.

_____

5 In a few years, people will have the ability to buy anything they want without leaving their homes.

_____

4 Complete the sentences with the correct form of *be able to*.

1 Fortunately, last year our organization _____ give $100,000 to food aid organizations.

2 We think that next year we _____ give even more.

3 However, most organizations _____ (not) do the same last year.

4 We're hoping they _____ increase their contributions in future years.

5 If you _____ help us, please contact our organization.

May, might, and could: Possibility ▶8.3

5 Read the sentences. Is the possibility in the present or the future? Write *P* (present) or *F* (future).

___ 1 We may not need a new TV, but we want one.

___ 2 Wait a few months—they may lower the price.

___ 3 The store might not take purchases back without a receipt, so you should save it.

___ 4 The world could run out of energy sources one day.

___ 5 I could buy fewer electronics, but it's so hard.

6 Write the words in the correct order to make sentences.

1 could / your smartphone / you / for a week / give up

_____?

2 might / an / car / we / buy / electric

_____.

3 live / my / without / video games/ could not / brother

_____.

4 may / year / shopping / for / a / quit / I

_____.

5 online / you / that shirt / might / find

_____.

6 meet / we / at the store / could / you

_____.

Giving gifts ▶8.1

1 Read the pairs of words or phrases. Is the meaning similar or different? Write *S* (similar) or *D* (different).

1 impress, bore ____

2 latest, last ____

3 exchange, switch ____

4 trend, tradition ____

5 budget, financial plan ____

6 match, go with ____

7 refund, expense ____

8 brand, material ____

9 mix, copy ____

2 Match the questions with the answers.

1 What are you going to wear? ____

2 Do you follow the latest fashions? ____

3 Do you usually stay within your clothes budget? ____

4 Why does she wear so much black? ____

5 What trends are popular with teenagers? ____

6 Will they give you a refund? ____

7 Why are some clothes so expensive? ____

a Brand names can cost a lot more.

b Yes, usually. I'm careful about money.

c I don't really don't know. My kids are older now.

d Not really. I think good style lasts forever.

e No, but I can exchange it for something the same price.

f A suit. I want to impress them.

g Then she can mix and match everything.

Describing food ▶8.2

3 Match the beginnings and endings of the phrases.

1 a very sour ____ a potato chips

2 salty ____ b ingredients

3 tastes ____ c good recipe

4 a list of ____ d mildly spicy

5 this is a ____ e lemon

6 avoid raw ____ f meat

7 eat out at ____ g bread

8 bake ____ h restaurants

4 Complete the sentences with the words in the box.

bake	eat out	ingredients	raw
recipe	salty	spicy	sour

1 Eating _____ eggs can make you sick.

2 How many _____ do you need to make sushi?

3 Is the juice too _____? You can add some sugar.

4 My mother has a great _____ for chicken soup.

5 That shrimp is _____! My lips are burning.

6 I really like _____ food like chips and nuts.

7 Let's _____ some cookies today.

8 How often do you _____ for lunch?

VOCABULARY DEVELOPMENT: Prefixes ▶8.3

5 Match the prefixes with their meanings.

1 anti- ____ a not enough

2 over- ____ b too much

3 pre- ____ c in favor of

4 post- ____ d after

5 pro- ____ e against

6 under- ____ f before

6 Complete the sentences with the words in the box.

anti-consumer	overpriced	pre-tablet	postmodern
postwar	pro-growth	underpaid	

1 Governments are usually _____ and want the country to be strong financially.

2 Companies may have _____ practices that help businesses but hurt the customer.

3 For example, businesses may sell _____ products that people can't afford.

4 Companies might also have _____ and overworked employees.

5 I'm doing my presentation on _____ architecture, a style that began in the 1960s and focuses on how the outside of a building looks.

6 This style was a reaction in part to _____ construction in Europe in the 1940s and 1950s.

7 Research used to be more difficult in _____ days when we went to the library or computer lab!

READING: Practice

1 Read the article. Complete the sentence.

Fair trade is a way to _____.

Making Trade More Fair

If you buy goods like coffee or chocolate, you've probably bought fair-trade products. Fair trade benefits both producers and consumers. It has become increasingly popular as a way to solve the problem of underpaid workers in developing countries, while also providing high-quality products.

Fair-trade programs give products a certification, which ensures a fair price to producers and may also provide additional money for community projects like schools, healthcare, or environmental protection. Small-scale farmers with certification are able to get more money for produce such as coffee and cotton. Larger banana or tea farms can also get certification for providing good wages and safe conditions.

Fair trade can benefit the consumer also. Fair-trade products may not have brand names, but they are often made by hand, and are of better quality. They may use more natural ingredients, or are better tasting. Fair trade acts as a correction of pro-growth business policies that favor large companies over small ones. Critics say it's unclear how much farmers actually benefit from fair trade, and some think it reflects the interests of northern consumers rather than those of developing countries and farming communities. Others fear that fair-trade practices may cause goods to be overpriced. However, a slightly higher price may be worth it to help the small farmers in developing countries.

—Adapted from *The Concise Oxford Dictionary of Politics and International Relations*, 4th ed., edited by Garrett Brown, Iain McLean, and Alistair McMillan

2 Read the article again. List three groups that benefit from fair trade.

1 _____

2 _____

3 _____

3 Read the article again. Complete the sentences with information from the article.

1 Fair-trade products get a _____, which ensures a _____ for producers.

2 Fair-trade can provide money for projects like _____.

3 Small-scale farmers plant produce such as _____ and _____.

4 Larger farms produce _____ and _____.

5 Fair-trade products may use _____ ingredients.

4 Read the article again. Are the statements True, False, or Not Given?

	True	False	Not Given
1 Underpaid workers are a problem in some countries.	☐	☐	☐
2 Any producer can claim to offer fair-trade products.	☐	☐	☐
3 Only small farms can be fair-trade producers.	☐	☐	☐
4 Fair-trade products are usually famous brand names.	☐	☐	☐
5 The largest number of fair-trade producers is in Africa.	☐	☐	☐
6 Fair-trade products are usually made by machine.	☐	☐	☐
7 There's some criticism of fair-trade.	☐	☐	☐
8 Sometimes fair-trade products are more expensive.	☐	☐	☐

READING SKILL: Interpreting visuals and data ▶8.2

5 Look at the pie chart. Match the products with the correct percentages.

Australia's Retail Sales of Fair-trade Products, 2015

other 2% cotton and sports products 1%
bananas 3%
tea 5%
coffee 34%   chocolate 55%

____	1	cotton and sports products	a	1%
____	2	coffee	b	2%
____	3	tea	c	3%
____	4	chocolate	d	5%
____	5	bananas	e	34%
____	6	other products	f	55%

6 Look at the pie chart in Exercise 5 again. Choose *True*, *False*, or *Not Given*.

		True	False	Not Given
1	Australia has a fair-trade program.	☐	☐	☐
2	Most of Australia's retail sales are of fair-trade products.	☐	☐	☐
3	The chart shows data for ten years.	☐	☐	☐
4	In 2015, coffee made up the largest percentage of fair-trade products sold.	☐	☐	☐
5	The smallest percentage sold was cotton and sports products.	☐	☐	☐
6	Australia has a larger fair-trade program than other countries.	☐	☐	☐
7	There is more fair-trade tea sold than bananas.	☐	☐	☐
8	Other fair-trade products include strawberries.	☐	☐	☐

7 Look at the table. Complete the sentences with information from the table.

Fair Trade: Facts and Figures	
# of farmers and workers in fair-trade certified producer organizations	1.66 million
average size of a fair-trade plot of land	1.4 hectares
# of fair-trade producer organizations	1,240
# of countries with fair-trade organizations	75
revenue generated by fair-trade sales in 2014–2015	$1.6 billion

1 There are 1,660,000 _____ in fair-trade certified producer organizations.

2 The average size of a fair-trade plot of land is _____ hectares.

3 There are _____ fair-trade producer organizations.

4 Fair-trade organizations are in 75 _____.

5 Fair-trade retail sales generated _____ dollars in revenues in 2014–2015.

REAL-WORLD ENGLISH: Making requests and confirming acceptance ▶8.4

1 Complete the conversations from the video with the words in the box.

| a tea | Can I sit | Can you get | get the sugar | I'll leave |
| no problem | OK | Right | Sure | you go |

CONVERSATION 1

Kevin: Hey, guys…Sorry I'm late. I haven't even had a coffee yet. ¹_____

my laptop here while I get one, ²_____?

Andy: ³_____. We'll be here.

Max: OK, ⁴_____.

Andy: Actually…Kevin? ⁵_____ me a coffee, too?

Max: Oh, yeah. Could you get me ⁶_____?

CONVERSATION 2

Kevin: Here ⁷_____, guys.

Andy: Oh…while you're up, ⁸_____ from over there! Thanks.

Kevin: ⁹_____.

Andy: Oh…could you get some milk, too? Sorry!

Kevin: Here it is. ¹⁰_____ down now, please?

Andy: Be my guest!

2 Read the expressions. What are their functions? Check *Request*, *Hesitating*, *Confirming*, or *Conditions*.

	Request	Hesitating	Confirming	Conditions
1 Uh, I guess so.	☐	☐	☐	☐
2 Yeah, but do you have any money?	☐	☐	☐	☐
3 Could you possibly get me some more tea?	☐	☐	☐	☐
4 Are you sure?	☐	☐	☐	☐
5 Really? That's what you want?	☐	☐	☐	☐
6 Would you mind moving over a seat?	☐	☐	☐	☐
7 Um, yes, I can certainly try.	☐	☐	☐	☐
8 Of course. If you could just give me a minute.	☐	☐	☐	☐

3 Complete the conversation with expressions from Exercise 2.

Server: I'm so sorry, but we have to fit another table in here.

¹_____?

Customer: ²_____.

Server: Absolutely. Thanks so much. Can I get you anything else?

Customer: ³_____

Server: Is that all? ⁴_____?

Customer: Well, I'd love this recipe. Could you ask the chef?

Server: ⁵_____, but she doesn't like to share

her recipes.

UNIT REVIEW: Podcast

> Go online and listen to the podcast from the Unit Review.

1 🔊 Listen to the Unit Review Podcast. What two types of shopping do they talk about?

2 🔊 Listen to the podcast again. Are the statements True, False, or Not Given?

		True	False	Not Given
1	Shopping behavior is shifting from stores to online.	☐	☐	☐
2	E-commerce is also called brick and mortar.	☐	☐	☐
3	Asians buy more online than South Americans.	☐	☐	☐
4	It's difficult to exchange online purchases.	☐	☐	☐
5	Young shoppers exchange more than older shoppers.	☐	☐	☐
6	Half of the shopping malls in North America are gone.	☐	☐	☐

3 🔊 Listen to the podcast again. How does Patel describe the two types of shopping? Write *S* (store) or *O* (online).

1 It used to be more popular than it is now. _____

2 People aged 18–34 prefer this. _____

3 A U.S. consumer makes 19 purchases this way each year. _____

4 You print a label, and a truck picks up your exchange. _____

5 People can see and touch products. _____

6 Shoppers can try things on. _____

LISTENING SKILL: Recognizing statements used as questions ▶8.1

4 🔊 Listen to the sentences from the podcast. Are the sentences statements or questions? Complete the sentences with the correct punctuation.

1 Could you tell us about the consumer trends you're following related to technology _____

2 Obviously, one of the biggest changes we've seen in shopping behavior related to technology is the shift from brick-and-mortar stores to e-commerce _____

3 By e-commerce, you mean online shopping _____

4 You say online shopping is becoming more popular _____

5 Can you explain what is driving this _____

6 You can find the brand names you want instantly, place an order, and schedule a delivery _____

7 So regular shopping malls are on the way out _____

DISCUSSION BOARD PREPARATION

5 Look at the Unit 8 Review Discussion Point. Read the questions in the prompt. Then read the reply. Why does the writer like to have the latest things?

_____

6 Overall, how does the writer feel about technology and consumerism?

_____

Unit 8 Consumption

55

Unit 8 Review Discussion Point

1   Read the quote. Think about the world we live in. In what ways are we happier because of the things we consume?
    "We used to build civilizations. Now we build shopping malls."
    —Bill Bryson, selected from *Oxford Dictionary of Humorous Quotations*, 4th ed., edited by Ned Sherrin
2   Are there any disadvantages of living in the consumer age?
3   How has technology changed consumption?

Latest: Hiro Kuratami
30 minutes ago
I think many people are happier because of the things they buy. For example, I really like to have the latest fashion or the newest phone. My things help me express who I am. Of course, I can't buy everything I want because I have to keep within a budget, so I shop carefully.

   Although it's easy to buy things nowadays, there are disadvantages of living in the consumer age. It might make us care more about things than about people. It can also cause money problems. For example, because it's so easy to shop online, people might buy more than they need. We're able to shop online at any time, and all we need is a laptop or a phone. This may cause us to spend too much money. Technology has changed consumption in other ways. Through social media we're able to see all of the things other people have. When I know my friends have a new video game, pair of sneakers, or car, I want them, too. I might feel bad because I don't have the same things. In general, I think technology encourages us to buy things we don't really need.

7 Overall, did the writer answer all the questions? If yes, explain. If no, what can the writer change? Then use the rubric to give a score for the reply. Give points: 0 (not successful)– 10 (successful).

Writing a Discussion Board Post	Points
The post answers the questions clearly and completely.	
The post has a general opening sentence and a general closing sentence.	
The post uses grammar and vocabulary from the unit.	
The post shows careful thinking about the topic.	
Sentences are complete and have correct punctuation.	
The post is long enough (180–220 words).	
Total	

WRITE YOUR POST

8 Read the quote. Think about the world we live in. In what ways are we happier because of the things we consume? Are there any disadvantages of living in the consumer age? How has technology changed consumption? Write a draft of your post for the Unit 8 Review Discussion Board.

"We used to build civilizations. Now we build shopping malls."
—Bill Bryson, selected from *Oxford Dictionary of Humorous Quotations*, 4th ed., edited by Ned Sherrin

9 Use the rubric from Exercise 7 to score your post. Then improve your post.

 Go ONLINE to add your comments to the discussion board.

9 Work

Zero and first conditional ▶9.1

1 Read the sentences. What kind of conditional is used? Write *0* (zero conditional) or *1* (first conditional).

____ 1 Wear nice clothes if you have an interview.

____ 2 If you practice first, you'll be more relaxed.

____ 3 You perform better if you're confident.

____ 4 If you're unprepared, they won't hire you.

____ 5 Job applicants are more successful if they know a lot about the company or organization.

____ 6 If she gets a job there, she might earn more.

2 Choose the correct words to complete the sentences.

1 The company is more likely to hire people if they *are / will be* confident.

2 *Smile / You'll smile* if you want to impress people.

3 I talk a lot in interviews if I *like / will like* the applicant.

4 The interviewer *calls / will call* tomorrow if they want me for a second interview.

5 If Luke doesn't ask questions, he *doesn't / might not* seem interested in the position.

Second conditional ▶9.2

3 Complete the second conditional sentences with the correct forms of the verbs in parentheses.

1 If you _____ (not, like) to travel, you _____ (hate) this job.

2 I _____ (apply) for the job if I _____ (be) you.

3 He _____ (move) if he _____ (get) the promotion.

4 If English _____ (not, be) so hard, we _____ (speak) it more fluently.

5 If she _____ (like) meeting people, she _____ (go) out more.

6 If they _____ (offer) more money, they _____ (have) more applicants.

4 Read the true situations. Then complete the sentences using the second conditional to talk about how the situations are unlikely or imaginary.

1 Jack doesn't have a job. He feels sad.

   If Jack had a job, he wouldn't feel sad.

2 I don't speak five languages. I'm not a translator.

   If I spoke _____.

3 I take computer programming. The company pays for our classes.

   I wouldn't take _____.

4 She doesn't have a choice. She travels a lot for work.

   If she had _____.

5 The job isn't perfect. It requires long hours.

   The job would be perfect _____.

6 They're independent. They don't need help.

   If they _____.

Reflexive pronouns ▶9.3

5 Write the correct subject pronouns for the reflexive pronouns.

1 myself _____   5 ourselves _____

2 themselves _____   6 himself _____

3 yourself _____   7 itself _____

4 herself _____

6 Complete the conversations with the correct reflexive pronouns.

1 A: Do you need help with that?

   B: No, thanks. I can do it _____.

2 A: Did you bake Anna's birthday cake?

   B: Actually, she made it _____.

3 A: Do they grow the food for the restaurant _____?

   B: Yes, they do. They have a garden nearby.

4 A: Linda and I are very proud of our food. We designed the menu _____.

   B: Very impressive. Do you cook it _____, too?

5 A: This letter says the applicant is a team player.

   B: Everyone describes _____ as a team player these days.

VOCABULARY

VOCABULARY DEVELOPMENT: Word building: Noun and adjective suffixes ▶9.1

1 Write the noun or adjective forms of the words.

1	appear	(noun)	_____
2	meaning	(adj)	_____
3	value	(adj)	_____
4	prepare	(noun)	_____
5	possible	(noun)	_____
6	move	(noun)	_____
7	negate	(adj)	_____
8	weak	(noun)	_____

2 Choose the correct words to complete the sentences.

1 Most teachers are very *active / action* and move around a lot.

2 To make a good *impressionable / impression*, smile and be *confident / confidence*.

3 Do you get a lot of *enjoyable / enjoyment* from your job?

4 This applicant writes a very *intelligent / intelligence* cover letter.

5 She has a lot of experience, but most of it isn't *applicable / application* to this position.

6 People who are *independent / independence* often work for themselves.

Personal skills ▶9.2

3 Rewrite the sentences using the words in the box.

artistic	capable	confident
determined	independent	

1 Are you able to do many things?

_____

2 Do you refuse to give up?

_____

3 Are you creative and imaginative?

_____

4 Can you work without help?

_____

5 We need someone who isn't shy.

_____

4 Complete the sentences with a word from Exercise 3.

1 Lena is _____, so she's taking a painting class.

2 Learning English isn't easy, but I'm _____ to do my best.

3 Henry likes to work alone. He's quite _____.

4 I'm taking a public speaking class so I will feel more _____ and less nervous about presentations.

5 Matt isn't _____ of fixing his car, so he took it to a garage.

Jobs ▶9.3

5 Read the pairs of words. Are their meanings similar or different? Write *S* (similar) or *D* (different).

1	temporary	permanent	____
2	fully	completely	____
3	highly	little	____
4	senior	junior	____
5	unlikely	possible	____
6	possible	potential	____

6 Complete the text with the words in the box.

highly	junior	permanent
senior	temporary	unlikely

Right now, I'm working as a desk clerk at a hotel, but I hope this is ¹_____. I'm interested in the hotel industry and realize I need to start in a more ²_____ position, but I plan to move up to manager one day. To get ³_____ employment in this field you need to be ⁴_____ qualified. As a desk clerk, I'm learning valuable skills that will help me be a successful candidate for any ⁵_____ management openings. It's ⁶_____ that I will get a promotion right away, but I am determined.

58

Unit 9 Work

1 Read the article. Complete the sentence.

The creative class is made up of people who _____.

Creative Class

In Richard Florida's theory of the creative class, the work that people do determines their position in the social and economic order. Creative class members are paid for their knowledge and ideas—their creativity. Physical work is no longer as useful as the work we do with our minds.

Creative class occupations include: science, engineering, and technology; business; healthcare, law, and education; and arts, entertainment, and media. They make up about 34 percent of all workers, with another 20 percent in factory or construction jobs, and more than 45 percent in service jobs like food preparation and retail sales. The creative class rose from 5 percent of all workers in 1900 to more than 30 percent by 2005. They generate half of all U.S. wages. Cities with a large creative class have

valuable characteristics, which Florida calls "the three Ts of economic development." The first "T" is technology. If a city has good universities, it is likely to have good technology. The second is talent. Skilled and educated workers include those who are artistic, capable, determined, and independent. The third "T" is tolerance, or openness. There will be movement of highly creative people to a city if it encourages an open-minded environment with all sorts of people. If a city wants to grow its creative class, it needs these three Ts.

—Adapted from *The Oxford Companion to American Politics* edited by David Coates

2 Read the article again. Are the statements True, False, or Not Given?

	True	False	Not Given
1 Florida thinks our social position determines our work.	☐	☐	☐
2 Creativity is now considered more useful than physical work.	☐	☐	☐
3 Architecture is a creative class occupation.	☐	☐	☐
4 Creative class occupations include retail sales.	☐	☐	☐
5 There are more creative class workers than anything else.	☐	☐	☐
6 There are 20 million factory and construction jobs.	☐	☐	☐
7 About 50% of all U.S. wages are generated by the creative class.	☐	☐	☐
8 Cities with a lot of creative workers have good technology.	☐	☐	☐

3 Read the article again. Complete the sentences with information from the article.

1 Florida's first name is _____.

2 In his theory, creativity is the same as _____.

3 Jobs in _____ make up the smallest group of workers.

4 _____ jobs make up the largest group of workers.

5 In 2005, _____ percent of jobs were in the creative class.

6 A city with _____ usually has good technology.

7 If you're open to new people and ideas, you have _____.

READING SKILL: Note-taking ▶9.1

4 Read the article again. Match the full word or phrase with a possible abbreviation.

1 creative   _____   a env.

2 economic position _____   b constr.

3 occupation   _____   c tech

4 construction   _____   d prep.

5 preparation   _____   e occ.

6 technology   _____   f univ.

7 universities   _____   g creat.

8 environment   _____   h econ. pos.

5 Read the article again. Complete the notes.

1 _____ theory of creative class: _____ determines social and

economic position

2 People paid for _____

3 _____ less useful

4 Ex. of creative class occup: _____

5 Workers: _____ creative class, _____ factory/const.,

_____ food prep/_____

6 Creative class = 5% in _____ increased to _____ in 2005

7 Creative class = _____ wages/salaries in US

8 3 T's:

_____: good _____

_____: skilled and educated workers

(_____)

_____: openness

9 Open-minded environment ⟶ _____

6 Use your notes to write a summary of the article. Do not look back at the article.

_____

_____

_____

_____

_____

REAL-WORLD ENGLISH: Offering to help; rejecting and accepting offers ▶9.4

1 Complete the conversation from the video with the words in the box.

a big help	be great	Do you want	if you need
let me get	Oh, thanks	would you like	

Jenna: Ugh…what was I thinking?

Andy: Here, [1]_____ that for you.

Jenna: [2]_____, Andy.

Andy: [3]_____ this on the table?

Jenna: That would [4]_____. Thanks.

Andy: Wow…what's in there?

Jenna: Files for a case we are working on. I have to start them.

Andy: Cathy said I should work with you today. So, [5]_____ help, I'm available. Uh…[6]_____ me to help you sort?

Jenna: That would be [7]_____. Thanks!

2 Write the functions in the box next to the sentences.

accept	offer to help	offer again
refuse	refuse again	comment on the task

1 Are you sure? It looks like a lot to carry. _____

2 No, really, I can handle it. _____

3 Can I help you with that? _____

4 Really…I have a free hand. I'm happy to take a bag. _____

5 OK, then. Thanks! _____

6 No, thanks. I've got it. _____

3 Rewrite the sentences in Exercise 2 in the correct order to make a conversation.

A: _____

B: _____

A: _____

B: _____

A: _____

B: _____

LISTENING SKILL: Predicting while listening ▶9.3

1 You are going to listen to a podcast about the qualities of a good worker and of a good boss. Which of the following do you think the podcast will mention?

☐ fair   ☐ artistic   ☐ capable   ☐ thoughtful   ☐ calm

☐ determined   ☐ confident   ☐ independent   ☐ enthusiastic

2 🔊 Listen to the podcast. While you listen, decide which qualities in Exercise 1 the speakers will use to describe a good worker or a good boss. Write the words in the chart.

Good worker	Good boss

UNIT REVIEW: Podcast

🔘 **Go online to listen to the podcast from the Unit Review.**

3 🔊 Listen to the Unit Review Podcast again. Check your predictions.

4 🔊 Listen to the Unit Review Podcast again. Are the statements True, False, or Not Given?

	True	False	Not Given
1 Neeta and Adam work together.	☐	☐	☐
2 Neeta teaches at a university.	☐	☐	☐
3 Good employees need supervision.	☐	☐	☐
4 Good employees get additional training.	☐	☐	☐
5 Good bosses make their employees better.	☐	☐	☐
6 Good bosses protect their employees.	☐	☐	☐
7 Good bosses take credit for employees' work.	☐	☐	☐
8 Good bosses crititicize employee behavior to help them overcome weaknesses.	☐	☐	☐
9 It's important for good bosses to reward employees.	☐	☐	☐
10 One sign of a good boss is good listening skills.	☐	☐	☐

DISCUSSION BOARD PREPARATION

5 Look at the Unit 9 Review Discussion Point. Read the questions in the prompt. Then read the reply. What is the writer's opinion about the quote?

_____

6 What reasons does the writer give for her opinion about the quote?

_____

7 What qualities does the writer think a good employee should have? A good boss?

_____

Unit 9 Review Discussion Point

1 Read the quote. Do you agree?
"The person who knows HOW will always have a job. The person who knows WHY will always be his boss."
—Diane Ravitch, selected from *Oxford Essential Quotations*, 5th ed., edited by Susan Ratcliffe

2 In what ways are good employees and good bosses similar or different?

Latest: Jamila Ade
three hours ago
I don't agree with the quote for several reasons. First, many people know how to do something, but they don't necessarily have a job. The economy affects jobs as much or more than someone's knowledge. Also, I think bosses usually know both HOW and WHY a job is done. And last, the quote suggests that there is a big difference between the type of people who are workers and the type who are bosses.

I think good employees and good bosses are similar in some ways. They are both responsible, capable, determined, enthusiastic, and confident. Good employees need to be able to follow directions and listen to supervisors. But they also should be able to think for themselves and be a little independent. Good bosses have to be good at communication. If they listen well and explain things clearly, the workers will do a better job. If the boss is enthusiastic and hard-working, he or she is a good example for the employees. A good boss also needs to understand more about the job or the company, so they need to have advanced training or education.

8 Overall, did the writer answer all the questions? If yes, explain. If no, what can the writer change? Then use the rubric to give a score for the reply. Give points: 0 (not successful)–10 (successful).

Writing a Discussion Board Post	Points
The post answers the questions clearly and completely.	
The post has a general opening sentence and a general closing sentence.	
The post uses grammar and vocabulary from the unit.	
The post shows careful thinking about the topic.	
Sentences are complete and have correct punctuation.	
The post is long enough (180–220 words).	
Total	

WRITE YOUR POST

9 Read the quote. Do you agree? In what ways are good employees and good bosses similar or different? Write a draft of your post for the Unit 9 Review Discussion Board.

 "The person who knows HOW will always have a job. The person who knows WHY will always be his boss."
—Diane Ravitch, selected from *Oxford Essential Quotations*, 5th ed., edited by Susan Ratcliffe

10 Use the rubric from Exercise 8 to score your post. Then improve your post.

Go ONLINE to add your comments to the discussion board.

10 Information

The passive: Simple present and simple past ▶10.1

1 Choose the correct words to complete the sentences.

1 The new account *created / was created* two weeks ago.
2 I *use / am used* the titles of songs for my passwords.
3 Credit card information *often steals / is often stolen* by thieves.
4 Hackers *break in / are broken in* to websites and online accounts all the time.
5 A firewall *installs / is installed* on all the company computers.
6 The accounts *didn't check / weren't checked* regularly.

2 Rewrite the sentences using the passive.

1 Someone changed my password.

_____

2 Websites use security questions as another form of protection.

_____

3 They ask these questions to check users' identities.

_____

4 People often forget usernames and passwords.

_____

5 Someone deleted the information by accident.

_____

6 People stole my identity.

_____

A/an, the, and no article ▶10.2

3 Choose the correct options to complete the sentences.

1 I prefer *an / -* information that is visual.
2 *The / -* Internet connects people around *a / the* world.
3 *The people / - People* usually read *the / an* article online more quickly than one in print.
4 We saw *the / a* fascinating program on TV last night.
5 *The / An* easiest way to do *- / a* research is online.

4 Complete the text with *a/an, the,* or - (no article).

According to ^{1}____ researchers, there is ^{2}____ difference between reading ^{3}____ articles in print and ^{4}____ articles online. For one thing, online articles use more ^{5}____ visuals. People who read online are used to seeing ^{6}____ information in ^{7}____ charts, graphs, and pictures as well as in ^{8}____ words. This helps them read quickly. Articles on ^{9}____ Internet also often have ^{10}____ links to other Web pages. Readers will click on ^{11}____ link and start reading ^{12}____ new story. This means they often don't finish ^{13}____ first article.

Indefinite pronouns and adverbs ▶10.3

5 Match the indefinite pronouns and adverbs with the descriptions.

____ 1 anyone   ____ 5 no one
____ 2 anything   ____ 6 nowhere
____ 3 everybody   ____ 7 someone
____ 4 everything ____ 8 somewhere

a used in positive sentences to talk about all people
b means "it doesn't matter who"
c used to talk about a place, but not a particular one
d means "no person"
e used to talk about all things
f means "no place"
g used in negative sentences to talk about things
h used to talk about a person, but not a particular one

6 Complete the conversations with the indefinite pronouns in the box.

anyone	anything	anywhere	nobody
something	everyone	everywhere	

1 A: Does _____ have a pen? I have to write _____ down.
   B: Yeah, here's one. Do you need _____ else?
2 A: I don't know _____ to look for news about the fire.
   B: Are you kidding? Look online—it's _____!
3 A: Where is _____? Did I get the time wrong?
   B: I don't know. _____ told me the time was changed.

Online safety ▶10.1

1 Choose the correct idioms to complete the sentences.

1 I sometimes use place names as passwords. *After all,* / *For instance,* my bank password is *Cuba*.

2 You should write the instructions down *for instance* / *in case* you forget.

3 Is it a good idea to have one password for everything? *All the time* / *Of course not*!

4 I review my privacy settings often. *Right now* / *All the time*, they are very private.

5 It's all right to give you the password. *After all* / *For instance*, we're on the same team.

6 Did your account get hacked? *Of course not* / *Too bad*.

2 Complete the conversations with the idioms in the box.

for instance	all the time	in case
of course not	right now	too bad

1 A: You lost all your files? That's _____!

  B: Yes, but I emailed them to myself just

  _____ something like this

  happened.

2 A: Do you save your credit card information on any

  websites?

  B: _____! People might find it and use

  it. _____, someone might charge a

  lot of stuff to my account.

3 A: I post photos on social media sites

  _____. Do you?

  B: No, never. It's hard to keep photos completely

  private _____.

VOCABULARY DEVELOPMENT:
Intensifying adverbs ▶10.2

3 Match the adverbs with the uses. You will use some letters more than once.

1 completely ____ a use with emotions

2 deeply ____ b use in all contexts

3 extremely ____ c with probability words

4 firmly ____ d with opinions or beliefs

5 really ____

6 strongly ____

4 Choose the correct words to complete the sentences.

1 We are *really* / *strongly* worried about Internet safety.

2 Lisa is *extremely* / *absolutely* certain that social media is dangerous.

3 The accident affected me *very* / *strongly*.

4 It's *firmly* / *extremely* unlikely that someone stole your identity.

5 I *very* / *deeply* admire people who help others.

6 We *deeply* / *completely* support that approach.

"Fake news" ▶10.3

5 Match the words or phrases with the meanings.

____ 1 accurately ____ 5 make something up

____ 2 claim ____ 6 proof

____ 3 freedom ____ 7 spread

____ 4 genuine ____ 8 trust

a believe in the truth of

b evidence establishing a fact or the truth of something

c exactly, in a way that is correct in all details

d real, truly what something is said to be

e cause to reach a wider audience or group of people

f state that something is true, usually without evidence

g invent a story, lie, or plan

h the power or right to act, speak, and think as one wants

6 Complete the text with the correct forms of the words and phrases in Exercise 5.

Who creates fake news and why? Many people

¹_____ stories for the money. They ²_____

ridiculous things are true on various websites. Advertisers

pay them each time a reader clicks on the article. Readers

don't realize that the news is not ³_____. They

share it on social media, and the false news ⁴_____.

Sometimes they create fake photographs as ⁵_____

that something is true. With technology, it's very easy

to fake a photo. I used to ⁶_____ that all articles

described events ⁷_____, but not anymore. I'm not

sure people should have the ⁸_____ to say whatever

they want.

VOCABULARY

READING: Practice

1 Read the article. Complete the sentence.

Multimedia is _____.

 ## Art and Multimedia

| Home | About | **Articles** |

Right now, multimedia is completely changing the art world. In multimedia, sound, graphics, video, text, and animation are combined to present interactive stories, games, and educational materials. Electronic storage (saving to "the cloud") allows symphonies, films, and even whole museums to exist online. The interactive nature of multimedia requires user participation, making it an extremely powerful tool for education and communication. Because of its interactivity and openness, multimedia challenges the idea of art having just one creator.

Interactivity is a key feature of digital multimedia. In the 1980s, the personal computer enabled artists to combine media. In the 1990s, multimedia spread to video games, educational programs, museum tours, and real estate guides. Interactivity is not only fun, it also changes the relationship between the artist and the viewer. Traditionally, art is given to a passive audience, but interactive multimedia gives everyone the freedom to make choices.

The use of multimedia is not problem-free. Because of its flexibility, it's difficult for people to trust that the content—digital photos, video, text, and music—is genuine. They can all easily be altered. For example, film studios currently use digital technology, and in seconds, night scenes can be converted to day scenes. And while cooperation and sharing between artists can be productive, the possibility of content theft is deeply troubling.

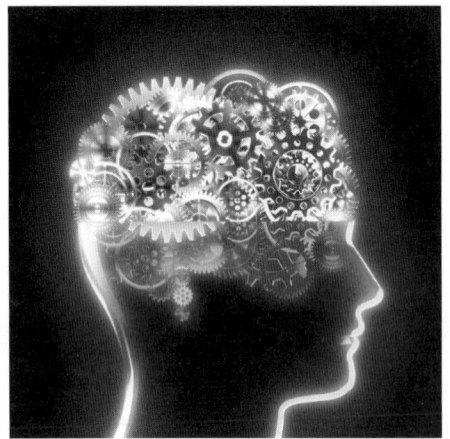

—adapted from *Encyclopedia of Aesthetics*, 2nd ed., edited by Michael Kelly

2 Choose the three main ideas.

☐ Multimedia is completely changing the art world.

☐ Electronic storage (saving to "the cloud") allows symphonies, films, and even whole museums to exist online.

☐ Interactivity is a key feature of digital multimedia.

☐ In the 1990s, multimedia spread to video games, educational programs, museum tours, and real estate guides.

☐ Interactivity is not only fun, it also changes the relationship between the artist and the viewer.

☐ Because of its flexibility, it's difficult to for people to trust that the content—digital photos, video, text, and music—is genuine.

☐ For example, film studios currently use digital techology, and in seconds, night scenes can be converted to day scenes.

3 Read the article again. Are the statements True, False, or Not Given?

	True	False	Not Given
1 Stories are an example of multimedia.	☐	☐	☐
2 User participation makes multimedia a powerful tool.	☐	☐	☐
3 Multimedia is used more for fun than education.	☐	☐	☐
4 Video games used multimedia in the 1980s.	☐	☐	☐
5 Museum tours use multimedia.	☐	☐	☐
6 The audience for art is less passive with multimedia.	☐	☐	☐
7 People are able to trust multimedia more.	☐	☐	☐
8 It's easier to change films than to change music.	☐	☐	☐

READING SKILL: Understanding pronoun references ▶10.2

4 Read the sentences from the article. What noun does the underlined pronoun refer to? Look at the article again as needed. Choose the correct options.

1 The interactive nature of multimedia requires user participation, making it an extremely powerful tool for education and communication.
   a interactive nature   b user participation   c powerful tool

2 Because of its interactivity and openness, multimedia challenges the idea of art having just one creator.
   a multimedia   b idea   c creator

3 Interactivity is not only fun, it also changes the relationship between the artist and the viewer.
   a multimedia   b fun   c interactivity

4 Because of its flexibility, it's difficult to for people to trust that the content—digital photos, video, text, and music—is genuine.
   a flexibility   b multimedia   c use

5 They can all easily be altered.
   a digital photos, video, text, music   b film studios   c people

5 Read the sentences. Write the word or words that the underlined pronouns refer to in the sentences.

1 Multimedia includes animation, music, and graphics. They can be combined in different ways. _____

2 Artists were considered the only creators of art, but with multimedia, they share this role with the audience. _____

3 Electronic storage (saving to the "cloud") allows a lot of information to be stored online. With it, museums and libraries don't need as much physical space. _____

4 Multimedia art uses interactivity to keep the user more completely engaged with it.

   _____

5 I don't understand the way that multimedia changes the role of the artist. Can you explain it? _____

6 Filmmakers can change scenes and the way they look with the use of computers.

   _____

REAL-WORLD ENGLISH: Giving and responding to feedback ▶10.4

1 Complete the conversation from Scene 1 of the video with the words in the box.

do you mean	poorly organized	really
to be honest	well	you should

Andy: ¹_____ make more eye contact.

Max: What ²_____? I was looking at you.

Andy: But you were looking at your notes more.

Max: ³_____ I haven't, er, memorized it yet.

Andy: And it's ⁴_____.

Max: ⁵_____? Are you sure?

Andy: ⁶_____, it's boring in places.

2 Complete the conversation from Scene 2 of the video with the words in the box.

check	great points	great presentation	excellent
more feedback	more information	sure	

Kevin: ¹_____. Andy thought so, too.

Max: Huh! Well, now it's time for ²_____ on our grant proposals!

Kevin: Oh, here's Emma.

Emma: Hi, Kevin. Max.

Max: So…

Emma: So, Kevin, You made a lot of ³_____, but ⁴_____ your sentence length, OK?

Kevin: Oh! OK! ⁵_____. Thanks.

Emma: Max…your idea is ⁶_____, but you need to give ⁷_____ on how the art project would help the community.

3 Look at the photo. Read the conversation and answer the questions.

Gisela: What do you think of my costume?

Anita: Hmm. It will definitely attract attention, but I think it could be more effective.

Gisela: Really? What do you mean?

Anita: Well, the white doesn't show up very well. And it looks really basic.

Gisela: I didn't have a lot of time. And I think it's good enough.

Anita: OK. Do what you want. I just think it's boring right now. From behind, it looks like a box on your head.

1 Who gives feedback? _____

2 Does the feedback focus on positive or negative things? _____

3 Does the feedback include specific examples of errors? _____

4 How well is the feedback received? _____

5 What mistakes does each speaker make? _____

UNIT REVIEW: Podcast

 Go online to listen to the podcast from the Unit Review.

1 Listen to the Unit Review Podcast. Are the statements True, False, or Not Given?

	True	False	Not Given
1 It's better to use search engines for research.	☐	☐	☐
2 Online searches about health problems are usually helpful.	☐	☐	☐
3 People can change search engine results by creating links.	☐	☐	☐
4 More people use search engines than go to the library.	☐	☐	☐
5 Information online can be difficult to read.	☐	☐	☐
6 You can find original sources in libraries.	☐	☐	☐

2 Listen to the podcast again. Choose the correct answers to the questions.

1 What is Alisha Brand's job?
  a podcast host   b research librarian   c computer researcher
2 What percentage of search engine results for headaches are helpful?
  a 30%   b 50%   c 70%
3 What do online search engines use to create the search results?
  a linked websites   b original sources   c formulas
4 How many search engines do people have access to?
  a 2–3   b 4–5   c 10–15
5 What is one problem with Internet research that Brand mentions?
  a It's incomplete.   b It's confusing.   c There's too much.
6 What is one way information in a library is different from online?
  a It's higher quality.   b It's easier to find.   c It's not as genuine.

LISTENING SKILL: Focusing on key content words ▶10.1

3 Listen to part of the podcast again. Complete the text with the key content words you hear.

Well, in some situations, people "bomb" the search engine. They can ¹_____ the
²_____ by linking websites and key ³_____. If they ⁴_____ this
enough ⁵_____, a result is ⁶_____ to the ⁷_____ of the list, which means
you can't completely ⁸_____ it. And right now, users often have access to only four or
five ⁹_____. So those search engines still control what you ¹⁰_____.

DISCUSSION BOARD PREPARATION

4 Look at the Unit 10 Review Discussion Point. Read the questions in the prompt. Then read the reply. What does the writer say about how libraries are used nowadays?

_____

_____

5 What benefits of a library does the writer mention?

_____

_____

Unit 10 Review Discussion Point

1 Read the quote. Will libraries disappear completely one day, or will they once again become a popular place to go for information?
  "*Google can bring you back 100,000 answers. A librarian can bring you back the right one.*"
  —Neil Gaiman, selected from *Oxford Essential Quotations*, 5th ed., edited by Susan Ratcliffe

2 What benefits do libraries provide that search engines do not?

Latest: Madhuri
one hour ago
I think libraries as we know them will disappear one day. We will still save books and papers in special places as a way to back up our electronic storage. It's possible that a terrible computer virus will wipe out all the data around the world, and we need to save that information. However, I think regular libraries will be very different. Now people still go to the library sometimes to get a book or read a magazine article. I think in the future, people will go to libraries to work, like they work in coffee shops now. People like to meet and work with others. We will also need librarians or other professionals to make sure we can trust the information we find online.
    Libraries have many benefits. Librarians know a lot about the information in libraries, and they can help us find the information we need. Physical books and documents are not as easy to change as the information on the Internet, so they are more genuine and we can trust them more. The original documents are also sometimes easier to read. Also, when I read information online, I don't remember it as well.

6 Overall, did the writer answer all the questions? If yes, explain. If no, what can the writer change? Then use the rubric to give a score for the reply. Give points: 0 (not successful)– 10 (successful).

Writing a Discussion Board Post	Points
The post answers the questions clearly and completely.	
The post has a general opening sentence and a general closing sentence.	
The post uses grammar and vocabulary from the unit.	
The post shows careful thinking about the topic.	
Sentences are complete and have correct punctuation.	
The post is long enough (180–220 words).	
Total	

WRITE YOUR POST

7 Read the quote. What does it mean? Will libraries disappear completely one day, or will they once again become a popular place to go for information? What benefits do libraries provide that search engines do not? Write a draft of your post for the Unit 10 Review Discussion Board.

"*Google can bring you back 100,000 answers. A librarian can bring you back the right one.*"
—Neil Gaiman, selected from *Oxford Essential Quotations*, 5th ed., edited by Susan Ratcliffe

8 Use the rubric from Exercise 6 to score your post. Then improve your post.

 Go ONLINE to add your comments to the discussion board.

11 Stories

Past perfect ▶11.1

1 Complete the sentences with the past perfect form of the verb in parentheses.

1 He _____ (call) a taxi to pick him up.

2 I _____ (not, eat) anything.

3 The snow _____ (begin) to fall.

4 Stores _____ (close) for the day.

5 We _____ (not, buy) any groceries.

6 My mother _____ (go) to the mall.

2 Correct the sentences using the past perfect.

1 She didn't received the letter.

_____

2 They had knew the man a long time.

_____

3 I'd lose the address.

_____

4 It hasn't stopped raining by 10:00 last night.

_____

5 We'd wrote a note.

_____

Simple past and past perfect ▶11.2

3 Read the sentences. Does the underlined event happen first or second? Write *1* or *2* on the line.

1 The show hadn't started when we arrived. ____

2 I'd already gone to bed when you called. ____

3 Although Mei had invited us, she wasn't there. ____

4 When the news was announced, we had gone. ____

5 After the police had questioned us, they left. ____

6 Before the accident happened, the traffic light had changed. ____

7 When the fire started, everyone ran for the doors. ____

4 Complete the sentences with the past perfect or simple past forms of the verbs in parentheses.

1 We _____ (open) the windows after the rain _____ (stop).

2 He _____ (already, buy) new clothes by the time they _____ (find) his luggage.

3 Rosa _____ (not, fly) before, so she _____ (be) scared.

4 I _____ (not, recognize) her because I _____ (not, meet) her before.

5 When Jason _____ (arrive), his friends _____ (already, leave).

Defining relative clauses ▶11.3

5 Read the sentences. Does the underlined noun refer to the subject or object of the relative clause? Write *S* or *O*. Then cross out any relative pronouns that aren't necessary.

____ 1 She likes books that have happy endings.

____ 2 Movies that are about the future are often expensive to make.

____ 3 Actors who I admire are rarely famous movie stars.

____ 4 I'm interested in the stories that people tell in other countries.

____ 5 He writes plots that create a lot of excitement.

6 Combine the sentences using the second sentences as defining relative clauses.

1 He is the author. He wrote *The Hobbit*.

He is the author who wrote The Hobbit.

2 I didn't like the movie. I saw it yesterday.

_____

3 Did you read the book? I gave it to you.

_____

4 Those movies are about scary situations. The situations frighten me.

_____

5 Meryl Streep is an actor. She's won many awards.

_____

6 Do you remember the director? We met him last year.

_____

VOCABULARY

VOCABULARY DEVELOPMENT: Verb + particle ▶11.1

1 Choose the correct words to complete the sentences.

1 When I _____ from my trip, I had a lot of work to do.

   a got away   b came back

2 How do you _____ problems with your boss?

   a work through   b keep away

3 When I _____ on my childhood, I remember how happy I was.

   a live through   b look back

4 Please _____. I don't want to get your cold!

   a keep away   b work through

5 My grandparents _____ times when they were very poor, so they are very careful with money.

   a looked back   b lived through

2 Think about how the particles are used. Choose the correct words to complete the sentences.

1 I own too many books, so I'm giving some *back / away*. Do you want one?

2 This is a difficult time, but I know you can get *away / through* it.

3 The accident was terrible to see. We had to look *away / back*.

4 When does Karina get *away / back* from her vacation?

5 The kids ran *away / back* when the old man caught them stealing his apples.

Fiction ▶11.2

3 Match the types of fiction with the descriptions.

____ 1 adventure   ____ 4 horror

____ 2 fantasy   ____ 5 romance

____ 3 historical fiction   ____ 6 thriller

a a love story

b exciting story about crime or disaster

c set in a past time

d a scary story

e often involves magic or imaginary worlds

f a story about a hero overcoming challenges

4 Choose the correct words to complete the sentences.

1 *Wolf Hall* is a(n) *horror / historical* novel in the time of King Henry VIII.

2 The Grimm brothers wrote *adventure stories / fairy tales* that included "Little Red Riding Hood."

3 I enjoy *adventures / fantasies* about the outdoors, such as stories about climbing Mount Everest.

4 Do you like stories that are set in the past or *fantasies / historical novels* about magical creatures?

5 I prefer happy stories like *romances / horrors*.

6 It's a *science fiction / thriller* story about astronauts living on Mars.

Movies ▶11.3

5 Match the phrases with the meanings.

____ 1 amusing plot   ____ 4 opening scene

____ 2 leading role   ____ 5 real highlight

____ 3 natural talent   ____ 6 recent release

a a movie that hasn't been in theaters long

b an ability to do something well without training

c one of the most important characters in a movie

d a funny story

e the first setting and action in a movie

f one of the best things

6 Complete the text with the correct form of a phrase from Exercise 5.

Nora Ephron wrote books and movies, including *When Harry Met Sally* and *Sleepless in Seattle*. Ephron seemed to have a ¹_____ for romantic comedies—love stories with ²_____. Ephron died in 2012, so she hasn't had any ³_____. In fact, her last film was *Julie and Julia* in 2009. Meryl Streep played one of the ⁴_____ in that movie, the famous chef Julia Child. In the ⁵_____, a woman is at her boring job answering phones. She decides to learn to cook. The food is a ⁶_____ of this movie. It will make you hungry!

REAL-WORLD READING

1 Read the section of a novel, *Anne of Green Gables*, which describes the adventures of 11-year-old Anne Shirley. Complete the sentence about the excerpt.

Matthew takes Anne home because _____.

Anne of Green Gables

Matthew Cuthbert and his sister Marilla decide to adopt an orphan[1]. They had requested a boy to help with the farm work, but when Matthew arrived at the station, he found they had sent a little girl instead.

She was about eleven, with long red hair in two plaits. Her face was small, white and thin, with a lot of freckles, and she had large grey-green eyes. She was wearing an old brown hat and a dress which was too small for her.

"Are you Mr. Cuthbert of Green Gables?" she asked excitedly in a high, sweet voice. "I'm very happy to come and live with you, and belong to you. I've never belonged to anyone, you see. The people at the children's home were very kind, but it's not very exciting to live in a place like that, is it?"

Matthew felt sorry for the child. How could he tell her that it was all a mistake? But he couldn't just leave her at the station. He decided to take her home with him. Marilla could explain the mistake to her.

He was surprised that he enjoyed the journey home. He was a quiet, shy man, and he didn't like talking himself. But today, he only had to listen, because the little girl talked and talked and talked.

—Extract from *Anne of Green Gables* by L. M. Montgomery

[1] orphan: a child whose parents have died

2 Complete the sentences with information from the story in Exercise 1.

1 The man's name is _____.

2 The girl's name is _____.

3 The place where the man lives is called _____.

4 He works on a _____.

5 His sister's name is _____.

6 The girl used to live at _____.

3 Read the story again. Are the statements True, False, or Not Given?

	True	False	Not Given
1 The man had asked for a boy.	☐	☐	☐
2 They wanted a boy to help with the store.	☐	☐	☐
3 The girl has no parents.	☐	☐	☐
4 She has two sisters.	☐	☐	☐
5 The children's home had 300 children living there.	☐	☐	☐
6 He tried to explain that it was a mistake.	☐	☐	☐
7 He said he would bring her back the next day.	☐	☐	☐
8 The man enjoys talking.	☐	☐	☐

READING SKILL: Analyzing characters in literary texts ▶11.2

4 Read the story again. Complete the sentences with the information from the story.

1 Anne was about _____ years old.

2 She had _____ hair, a _____ face, a lot of

_____, and _____ eyes.

3 She was wearing _____.

4 Her voice is _____.

5 Anne thought the people at the children's home were _____, but living

there was _____.

6 Matthew felt _____ for Anne.

7 Matthew is unlike Anne because _____.

8 On the way home, Matthew feels _____.

5 Look at your answers from Exercise 4. Choose the best words to complete the sentences.

1 Her appearance suggests _____.

  a she might not eat a lot   b she was very healthy

  c she was big for her age

2 Her clothing suggests _____.

  a she shopped a lot   b she liked to wear pants

  c she didn't have a lot of clothes

3 Her appearance and words suggest _____.

  a her life has been easy   b she has traveled a lot   c she's had a hard time

4 Her voice and words suggest _____.

  a she's often sad   b she's cheerful   c she isn't very smart

5 Anne's actions suggest _____.

  a she's afraid of Matthew   b she's friendly   c she's shy

6 Matthew's actions suggest he _____.

  a works hard   b has a lot of money   c is kind

7 His decision to let Marilla explain suggests _____.

  a she is nicer than he is   b she is older than he is

  c he doesn't like to cause problems

8 Matthew's feelings on the ride home suggest _____.

  a he likes Anne   b he doesn't like children

  c he likes to go into town

REAL-WORLD ENGLISH: Interrupting a conversation ▶11.4

1 Match the beginnings of the expressions from the video in *A* with the endings in *B*.

A		B	
1	Do you have ____	a	to go.
2	Sorry to ____	b	can…
3	It's okay. I ____	c	talking about…
4	I have ____	d	that, Max.
5	Sorry about ____	e	a minute?
6	Sorry, can ____	f	talk to you about something?
7	Excuse me. Can I ____	g	I just say something?
8	We were just ____	h	interrupt.

2 Answer the questions about the expressions in Exercise 1. Write the item number(s) on the line.

1 Which expressions are indirect ways to interrupt? ____

2 Which expression is a direct way to interrupt? ____

3 Which expression is a way to allow the other person to continue without interruption? ____

4 Which is an apology for being unavailable at first? ____

5 Which expression is a way to let someone know that he or she is interrupting? ____

3 Choose the best expressions in the conversations.

1 A: 1 *Excuse me, Professor. Do you have a minute?*
     2 Wait, Professor!
  B: Of course, Sara. What is it?

2 A: So, first I'll give the summary, and then Mike will go over the kinds of movies, and Ken, you…
  B: 1 *Hold on! Shouldn't we start with an introduction?*
     2 Excuse me. Could I interrupt you for a moment?

3 A: Talia, I'd like to go over the sales report before the meeting on Friday.
  B: 1 *Look, I've gotta go.*
     2 Excuse me. Could we continue this conversation tomorrow? I have an appointment.

4 A: 1 *I'm sorry, but could I say something? Peanut butter will make me really sick.*
     2 Wait—don't add the peanut butter! I'll get really sick.
  B: Oh, wow! Sorry, Lisa! Glad you stopped me in time.

5 A: If you could just complete these forms, I'll get that…
  B: 1 *I'm really sorry, but could I get some information first?*
     2 Hold on. I have a question.

4 Choose one conversation from Exercise 3. Who are the people? Is it a formal or informal situation? How can you tell?

_____

_____

ENGLISH FOR REAL

UNIT REVIEW: Podcast

Go online to listen to the podcast from the Unit Review.

1 Listen to the Unit Review Podcast. Check the types of fiction you hear.

☐ fantasy   ☐ historical fiction   ☐ adventure
☐ romance   ☐ thriller   ☐ horror
☐ science fiction   ☐ fairy tale   ☐ mystery

2 Listen to the podcast again. Who says it? Write J (Jason) or M (Min).

1 The plot is really important. ——

2 They end best when something a little surprising happens. ——

3 I can often work through the solution ahead of time if I read carefully. ——

4 But I also like novels that end in a completely unexpected way. ——

5 The couple always ended up together. ——

6 An ending doesn't have to be dramatic. ——

7 I thought about it for days. ——

8 Most readers enjoy a story as much or more when they know how it will end. ——

LISTENING SKILL: Recognizing linking with consonants ▶11.1

3 Listen to the sentences from the podcast. Where do you hear linking with consonants? Choose the correct options.

1 I don't know if there is one best technique for ending a story.
   a don't know   b if there   c best technique
2 I can often work through the solution ahead of time if I read carefully.
   a I can   b work through   c ahead of
3 But I also like novels that end in a completely unexpected way.
   a But I   b also like   c novels that
4 For example, I used to read romances.
   a example I   b used to   c read romances
5 I thought about it for days.
   a I thought   b thought about   c for days
6 Maybe that's why I enjoy reading stories over and over again.
   a Maybe that's   b why I   c and over

DISCUSSION BOARD PREPARATION

4 Look at the Unit 11 Review Discussion Point. Read the questions in the prompt. Then read the reply. What kind of story ending does the writer like?

_____

5 What examples does the writer give of stories where the ending should be changed?

_____

Unit 11 Review Discussion Point

1 Read the quote. What makes a good ending for a story?
"The good ended happily, and the bad unhappily. That is what fiction means."
—Oscar Wilde, selected from *Oxford Dictionary of Quotations*, 8th ed., edited by Elizabeth Knowles
2 Do you ever read ahead to find out what happens?
3 Are there any stories you know where you would like to change the ending?

Latest: Jean
one day ago
I think an ending should be a little surprising, but not too unexpected. I don't want to predict exactly how the story will go. It needs to make sense, but give me something to think about. In general, I like happy endings, or at least one that gives me a little hope. An adventure should end with a successful return, and a romance should end with the couple getting together, or at least being happier. I think a thriller should end with the bad people receiving justice.
   I sometimes read ahead to find out what happens. For example, if I think something bad might happen, I look at the ending to see if everything is OK. Even with mysteries, I sometimes like a clue as to how things turn out. Some endings are disappointing. For example, in *Alice in Wonderland* you find out at the very end that the entire story was just a dream. In many stories, a favorite character dies, and I'm often upset. For example, in the Harry Potter books, I did not like it when Professor Dumbledore died.

6 Overall, did the writer answer all the questions? If yes, explain. If no, what can the writer change? Then use the rubric to give a score for the reply. Give points: 0 (not successful)– 10 (successful).

_____

_____

Writing a Discussion Board Post	Points
The post answers the questions clearly and completely.	
The post has a general opening sentence and a general closing sentence.	
The post uses grammar and vocabulary from the unit.	
The post shows careful thinking about the topic.	
Sentences are complete and have correct punctuation.	
The post is long enough (180–220 words).	
Total	

WRITE YOUR POST

7 Read the quote. What makes a good ending for a story? Do you ever read ahead to find out what happens? Are there any stories you know where you would like to change the ending? Write a draft of your post for the Unit 11 Review Discussion Board.

"The good ended happily, and the bad unhappily.
That is what fiction means."
—Oscar Wilde, selected from *Oxford Dictionary of Quotations*, 8th ed., edited by Elzabeth Knowles

8 Use the rubric from Exercise 6 to score your post. Then improve your post.

 Go ONLINE to add your comments to the discussion board.

Unit 11 Stories

12 Emotion

Adjective + infinitive/infinitive of purpose ▶12.1

1 Complete the sentences with the correct forms of the verbs in the box. Some verbs may be negative.

be	get	hear	learn
listen	meet	prepare	win

1 He took classes _____ new skills.

2 It's important _____ to others' opinions.

3 It's hard _____ upset when people criticize you.

4 I'm exercising more _____ in shape.

5 She was very excited _____ the good news.

6 We were disappointed _____ the game.

7 They arrived early _____ for the presentation.

8 It's fun _____ new people.

2 Write the words in the correct order to make sentences with infinitives.

1 become / went / to / to / she / a / teacher / school

_____.

2 hard / to / about / not / the bad weather / it's / complain

_____.

3 parents / are / to / prepared / you / be

_____?

4 speeches / travels / give / lot / to / he / a

_____.

5 happy / my / of / help / most / are / to / friends

_____.

6 share / ideas / important / it's / to / your

_____.

Verb + *to* infinitive only ▶12.2

3 Choose the correct words to complete the sentences.

1 We agreed *to meet* / *meet* later.

2 She decided *to not* / *not to* study abroad.

3 I *hope to* / *hope* study abroad next year.

4 They planned *to work* / *work* together.

5 Alan seemed *like* / *to like* my suggestion.

6 I learned *not to trust* / *to not trust* my memory alone.

4 Match the beginnings and endings of the sentences.

1 I really _____   a sell their house soon.

2 Do you plan to _____   b to tell my secret.

3 It didn't fit, so I decided _____   c leave at 2:00?

     d not to buy it.

4 She promised not _____   e want to see the film.

5 They need to _____   f like to fix his car.

6 He says he'd _____

Verbs with the *-ing* form ▶12.3

5 Choose the correct words to complete the sentences.

1 I keep *to forget* / *forgetting* his name.

2 They arranged *to meet* / *meeting* tonight.

3 My favorite summer activity is going *to swim* / *swimming*.

4 He can't stand *to live* / *living* in a big city.

5 She promised *not to text* / *not texting* and drive.

6 We finished *to work* / *working* later than usual.

7 I can't imagine *not to have* / *not having* a good trip to Paris. It's such a great city!

6 Complete the text with the correct forms of the verbs in parentheses.

I've always enjoyed ¹_____ (learn) about other cultures, so I decided ²_____ (teach) in another country for a year. First, I had to stop ³_____ (worry) about all of the changes to my life. I wanted ⁴_____ (grow), so I had to do something new and different. Once I actually got to Swaziland, I realized I didn't mind ⁵_____ (meet) new people or ⁶_____ (change) old habits.

VOCABULARY DEVELOPMENT:
Vague language ▶12.1

1 Is the underlined language vague? Choose *Yes* or *No*.

		Yes	No
1	I have a lot of <u>stuff</u> to throw away.	☐	☐
2	She moved there on <u>March 1</u>.	☐	☐
3	Anwar has many <u>things like that</u>.	☐	☐
4	<u>Something</u> happened to make him late.	☐	☐
5	Ian was <u>almost</u> in high school then.	☐	☐
6	<u>Marisol</u> told me about the conference.	☐	☐
7	The award is <u>kind of</u> a big deal.	☐	☐
8	The top three winners <u>receive $20,000</u>.	☐	☐

2 Complete the sentences with the best word or phrase in the box.

around	stuff	sort of
someone	somewhere	things like that

1 I left my _____ in your car.

2 Do you enjoy science and _____?

3 _____ said Ahmed was disappointed with his performance.

4 There were _____ a thousand people at the conference.

5 Alexa and I are going to meet _____ downtown before the show.

6 We're _____ nervous about the game.

Emotions ▶12.2

3 Match the emotions with the definitions.

____ 1 anxious   ____ 5 relaxed

____ 2 curious   ____ 6 satisfied

____ 3 guilty   ____ 7 welcome

____ 4 impatient

a a feeling that you belong, are well received

b eager to know or learn something

c having or showing a tendency to be quickly irritated

d free from tension or worry

e pleased

f showing worry or nervousness

g responsible for doing something wrong

4 Complete the sentences with the emotions from Exercise 3.

1 My hosts in Japan were so friendly. They made me feel very _____.

2 Leo is so _____! He's always asking questions and looking things up.

3 Before the test, I was very _____ because I failed the last one.

4 I was very _____ after doing yoga.

5 Were you _____ with the room, or did you have problems?

6 Greta felt _____ about making Diane cry.

7 This line is taking forever. I'm getting very _____.

Decisions ▶12.3

5 Read the pairs of words or phrases. Are their meanings similar or different? Write *S* or *D*.

1 calculate   figure out   ____

2 balance   concentration   ____

3 thinking   action   ____

4 value   ignore   ____

5 convince   persuade   ____

6 risk   danger   ____

6 Complete the sentences with the words in the box.

balance	calculate	convince
risk	thinking	value

1 Do you think you have a good work and life _____?

2 I didn't move away because I _____ my friends and family here too much to leave them.

3 Jamie took a _____ in accepting a job at a brand-new company.

4 If my math is correct, I _____ our vacation this year will cost less than last year.

5 How can I _____ you to come with us?

6 Marco's way of _____ is very different from mine.

VOCABULARY

READING: Practice

1 Read the article. Complete the sentence.

Two things that affect emotions are _____.

Emotions

Even though emotions are universal, they are also deeply affected by culture and historical context.

Early work on emotions focused particularly on western Europe and the United States. During the seventeenth and eighteenth centuries, people began to show less anger, particularly within the family. Also around that time, romantic love became more important, affecting marriage arrangements. At this time, although women largely stopped showing anger, men were encouraged to express appropriate anger, but not fear. In the twentieth century, feeling angry, guilty, anxious, fearful, or jealous was seen as harmful in U.S. society although it was okay to express some of these emotions through movies or sporting events.

Just as the expression of emotion changes over time, it also varies across cultures. Some societies, especially around the Mediterranean, value emotions surrounding respect; they also see anger, jealousy, and other similar feelings as positive. Interestingly, when jealous, Dutch people become sad, Frenchmen become angry, but Americans worry that jealousy reveals too much. According to one study, Chinese people value negative emotions, such as fear, more than other societies; Chinese people were much less likely, however, in the 1970s, to claim to experience love.

In the modern world, there are always variations in emotions. In addition, new ones appear, like the unusual U.S. commitment to self-confidence in children.

—Adapted from *Oxford Encyclopedia of the Modern World*, edited by Peter N. Stearns

2 Check the best statement of the main idea.

☐ Emotions are universal—in every time and culture.
☐ The expression of emotions changes over time and across cultures.
☐ In the past, some emotions were more popular than others.
☐ People in Europe and Asia are different in the way they feel emotions.

3 Read the article again. Are the statements True, False, or Not Given?

	True	False	Not Given
1 Early discussion of emotions focused on Africa and Asia.	☐	☐	☐
2 People showed less anger in the family during the 1700s.	☐	☐	☐
3 Romantic love has always been important in Europe.	☐	☐	☐
4 Anger is more common than sadness.	☐	☐	☐
5 Sporting events are an acceptable place to express negative emotions.	☐	☐	☐
6 In countries that value respect, jealousy is accepted.	☐	☐	☐
7 South Americans express more joy than Asians.	☐	☐	☐
8 Some cultures value fear, but others don't.	☐	☐	☐
9 Sometimes new emotions appear.	☐	☐	☐

READING SKILL: Recognizing contrast linking words ▶12.2

4 Read the sentences from the article. Do the linking words express contrast or add similar information? Check *C* (contrast), *S* (similar information), or *N* (no linking word).

	C	S	N
1 Even though emotions are universal, they are also deeply affected by culture and historical context.			
2 Early work on emotions focused particularly on Western Europe and the United States.			
3 During the seventeenth and eighteenth centuries, people began to show less anger, particularly within the family.			
4 Also around that time, romantic love became more important, affecting marriage arrangements.			
5 At this time, although women largely stopped showing anger, men were encouraged to express appropriate anger, but not fear.			
6 In the twentieth century, feeling angry, guilty, anxious, fearful, or jealous was seen as harmful in U.S. society although it was OK to express some of these emotions through movies or sporting events.			
7 Just as the expression of emotion changes over time, it also varies across cultures.			
8 Some societies, especially around the Mediterranean, value emotions surrounding respect; they also see anger, jealousy, and other similar feelings as positive.			
9 Interestingly, when jealous, Dutch people become sad, Frenchmen become angry, but Americans worry that jealousy reveals too much.			
10 According to one study, Chinese people value negative emotions, such as fear, more than other soceities; Chinese people were much less likely, however, in the 1970s, to claim to experience love.			
11 In the modern world, there are always variations in emotions.			
12 In addition, new ones appear, like the unusual U.S. commitment to self-confidence in children.			

5 Read the article again. Match the phrases that are contrasted with each other in the article.

1 emotions are universal _____ a men expressed appropriate anger

2 women stopped showing anger _____ b less likely to claim experience of love

3 negative emotions were seen as harmful _____ c affected by culture and historical context

4 The French get angry when jealous _____ d could be expressed through sporting events

5 Chinese people value negative emotions _____ e Americans think it reveals too much

6 men expressed appropriate anger _____ f they couldn't show fear

REAL-WORLD ENGLISH: Reacting to news ▶12.4

1 Complete the conversation from the video with the phrases in the box.

be amazing	found out	good for you	great news
OK	that's awesome	too bad	your email

Kevin: I just [1]_____ that I got one of the grant awards! For science!

Andy: Hey! [2]_____. You got the grant! [3]_____!

Max: That's [4]_____, Kevin. I'm really happy for you!

Kevin: Well, Max, you should hear about the art grant today! Check [5]_____.

Andy: Oh, that would [6]_____. Check it now!

Max: Mm. No…I didn't get anything.

Andy: Really? Aw, that's [7]_____, Max.

Max: Oh, it's [8]_____. I didn't expect it.

2 Answer the questions about the conversation in Exercise 1.

1 Does Kevin have good or bad news?

_____

2 Who shows excitement at his news?

_____

3 Who has bad news?

_____

4 Who shows sympathy? How?

_____

3 Read the news. Check *Good* or *Bad*.

		Good	Bad
1	Hey, Dan, I just got a job offer in London.	☐	☐
2	I wasn't able to finish the sales report. My cousin had surgery yesterday.	☐	☐
3	I got a terrible grade on the presentation. And I really did a lot of work on it.	☐	☐
4	We won our game. Sorry you had to miss it.	☐	☐
5	Excuse me, I just saw a terrible accident. I need to sit down. Is this seat free?	☐	☐

4 Choose the best response to each piece of news in Exercise 3.

1 a Awesome! Way to go!
  b That's too bad.

2 a That's terrible. I'm very sorry to hear that.
  b No way! You're kidding!

3 a Don't worry about it.
  b You must be disappointed. Have you talked to Professor Golden?

4 a Oh, that's too bad.
  b Great! Wish I had been there!

5 a How awful! I'm so sorry to hear that. Of course, please sit.
  b That's too bad, dude.

Unit 12 Emotion

UNIT REVIEW: Podcast

 Go online to listen to the podcast from the Unit Review.

1 Listen to the Unit Review Podcast. Are the emotions positive or negative, according to the speakers?

		Positive	Negative
1	amusement, amused	☐	☐
2	anger, angry	☐	☐
3	curiosity, curious	☐	☐
4	disgust, disgusted	☐	☐
5	fear, afraid	☐	☐
6	guilt, guilty	☐	☐
7	happiness, happy	☐	☐
8	satisfaction, satisfied	☐	☐

2 Listen to the podcast again. Choose the correct options to complete the sentences.

1 In general, the podcast is about _____.

   a happiness   b anger   c disgust

2 Alan Park writes about _____ of negative emotions.

   a disadvantages   b differences in   c positive aspects

3 Fear can help us _____.

   a become brave   b avoid danger   c be lonely

4 We are happier when we feel _____ emotion we want to feel.

   a a pleasant   b an unpleasant   c any

5 According to the podcast, making facial expressions can _____.

   a hurt others   b make you more positive   c make you more angry

LISTENING SKILL: Recognizing intonation in exclamations ▶12.3

3 Listen to the exclamations from the podcast. Match the exclamations with the meanings.

1	Welcome!	____	a	There's no doubt that's true.
2	Surprisingly, there is!	____	b	That's a relief!
3	You're kidding!	____	c	That's amazing.
4	Absolutely!	____	d	It might shock you, but it's true.
5	Phew!	____	e	I'm glad you're here.

DISCUSSION BOARD PREPARATION

4 Look at the Unit 12 Review Discussion Point. Read the questions in the prompt. Then read the reply. What does the writer think about sharing feelings?

_____

5 What examples does the author give to show that sharing feelings is difficult?

_____

Unit 12 Review Discussion Point

1   Read the quote. In what ways is it important for people to share their feelings?
    "Laugh and the world laughs with you; weep and you weep alone."
    —Horace (65–8 BCE), selected from *Oxford Dictionary of Proverbs*, 6th ed., edited by Jennifer Speake
2   What are the difficulties?
3   Are there any feelings people would rather not share?

Latest: Jamila Ade
three hours ago
I think it's important for people to share their feelings in many ways, or at least in many situations. If we don't share our feelings, it's hard to communicate or get close to people. When I'm happy and tell people, they often share my good feelings, and that makes me happier. And when I'm sad, other people can help me feel better.

However, sometimes sharing feelings causes problems. For example, if I tell someone that I am angry with them, they might be upset and not want to talk to me. Or, I might tell someone I'm feeling bad, and then I feel even worse because I've been honest, and they don't care or don't show any understanding or sympathy. Sharing feelings can be difficult.

Most people, in my opinion, don't like to share feelings that make them look bad or weak. Telling other people that you feel afraid or sad is very hard. Other people can sometimes judge you for your feelings. It is much easier to tell people you feel happy or amused or curious about something. But when you feel like you're not doing a good job at something, it is very difficult to share.

6 Overall, did the writer answer all the questions? If yes, explain. If no, what can the writer change? Then use the rubric to give a score for the reply. Give points: 0 (not successful)– 10 (successful).

_____

_____

Writing a Discussion Board Post	Points
The post answers the questions clearly and completely.	
The post has a general opening sentence and a general closing sentence.	
The post uses grammar and vocabulary from the unit.	
The post shows careful thinking about the topic.	
Sentences are complete and have correct punctuation.	
The post is long enough (180–220 words).	
Total	

WRITE YOUR POST

7 Read the quote. In what ways is it important for people to share their feelings? What are the difficulties? Are there any feelings people would rather not share? Write a draft of your post for the Unit 12 Review Discussion Board.

 *"Laugh and the world laughs with you; weep and you weep alone."*
—Horace (65–8 BCE), selected from *Oxford Dictionary of Proverbs*, 6th ed., edited by Jennifer Speake

8 Use the rubric from Exercise 6 to score your post. Then improve your post.

 Go ONLINE to add your comments to the discussion board.